Why Are We Here?

Discerning Our Unitarian Mission in an Upturned World

Commissioning Editor:

Jane Blackall

The Lindsey Press
London

the unitarians

Published by The Lindsey Press
on behalf of The General Assembly of
Unitarian and Free Christian Churches
Essex Hall, 1–6 Essex Street, London WC2R 3HY, UK

www.unitarian.org.uk

© The General Assembly of Unitarian and Free Christian Churches 2022

ISBN 978-0-85319-096-7

Designed and typeset by Garth Stewart

Contents

Foreword

I am glad that the Lindsey Press is able to publish a selection of the talks given at the 2021 Summer School, under the title *Why Are We Here? Discerning our Unitarian Mission in an Upturned World*. The prevailing coronavirus pandemic meant that the event had to be held online, instead of the usual residential week at the Nightingale Centre in the Peak District. That context rendered the question in the title all the more urgent. The virus has turned all our lives upside down, and the effects will continue to be felt even after the case numbers have declined.

But, as all the contributors to this collection urge, we need to be asking that question anyway. I am grateful to them, and to the organisers of the event, for bringing it to the fore amid the tumult of these times. As Jo James said in his talk, 'We must not be afraid of times of great change'. These are undoubtedly those times, both in our wider society and within our Unitarian movement. Pandemic, increasing social inequality, environmental damage, climate crisis, and political division dominate the news media every day. The long decline in membership of our movement has reached a critical level. There are congregations who did not know they were closing their doors for the last time when the pandemic began, and there are others who have realised that they can't continue in the same way as before. Meanwhile, these times of uncertainty are pushing more and more people to look to spiritual community and practice for support, guidance, and resilience, as the limits of the secular consumerist world become apparent.

In an upturned world we have a responsibility to respond, but also to lead. Our core Unitarian principles of freedom and inquiry mean that in meeting the spiritual needs of today we must evolve, keep questioning, keep seeking truth. We are not bound by traditional liturgy or ritual. Yes, we have our own habits and culture, but we don't lose our identity by letting them go. Leading in a time of uncertainty means risking getting it wrong, while paying attention to the need for 'discernment' that is indicated in the sub-title of this collection. Many of the challenges described by the contributors are the result of too little discernment, of being pulled by mainstream currents, or propelled by outdated habits, rather than acting in line with our true purpose.

For some, 'purpose' is a less tarnished word than 'mission', which, especially in this religious context, might be associated with overseas missionary work, and the oppression, dehumanisation, and cultural erasure that it often brought – as Shana Begum reminds us in her chapter. Instead, the 'mission' explored here is our Unitarian purpose, our commitment, our ministry – driven by conscience, by God, by love, by justice – depending on the language and framing that works for each of us. Jane Blackall shows us that 'Our mission, our purpose, our *why* will be rooted in our spiritual and moral vision', whether we are drawn to create 'the Kingdom of God' or 'a better world'.

This collection of texts declares the need for our collective imagination. As Rory Castle Jones puts it, 'I believe that our job, as people of faith, is to imagine the unimaginable'. By demonstrating this imagined future, we can inspire others to act: practising imagination as leadership.

The membership of our movement spans many generations, and many people originally came to Unitarianism in a cultural and religious context that no longer prevails and would not be recognised by younger people joining today. In answering the question 'Why are we here?', it is important to acknowledge this fact: as Jo James frames it, 'What are we doing right now?'. Our spiritual and moral vision may be essentially timeless, but it is important to check the cultural perspectives that condition it for us, and what that means for our engagement with others beyond our immediate circle.

Shana Begum's invitation to welcome diversity reveals some of the blind spots to which we are prone without an active aim to stay attuned to changing culture. 'Being welcoming' means more than just offering a seat at the existing table: it means allowing ourselves to change in response to new people and ideas. We must acknowledge the power dynamics that exist in our movement and how these play out.

In a British culture where many adults have grown up with little religious influence in their lives, yet hear widespread stories of abuse, misogyny, and homophobia in religious institutions, we need to explain clearly what we are doing and what we stand for. We can't assume that people have a lived experience of belonging to a spiritual community, that they will understand the value that ours can offer, or that they will know they will be welcomed. As Kate Brady McKenna says, 'We need to be there for people who are not used to having a church be there for them'.

Not included in this collection is Stephen Lingwood's Summer School presentation entitled 'On the Prophetic Mission in the Climate Crisis as the Cultivation of Resistance, Repentance, and Resilience'. I recommend it to you; audio and video versions of his talk (and all these talks) can be found on the Summer School website (www.hucklowsummerschool.co.uk/talks/), and an expanded version of Stephen's text will appear as a chapter in a forthcoming Lindsey Press volume on eco-spirituality.

In the words of Norbert Capek, quoted at the close of Kate Brady McKenna's talk, '*It is worthwhile to live and to fight courageously for sacred ideals*'. And in the words of Jacob Davies, quoted by Rory Castle Jones, '*This is the moment of choice*'. I hope you will find inspiration in these pages to find the way to your own choice in these upturned times.

Elizabeth Slade
Chief Officer, The General Assembly of Unitarian and Free Christian Churches
January 2022

1 Why *Are* We Here?

Jane Blackall

To say that we are living in an upturned world is a bit of an understatement. Many of us feel overwhelmed right now: both with grief at the sufferings of the world and all her people, and with our own daily struggles. Many are traumatised and exhausted, navigating loss, uncertainty, conflict, and hardship. Covid is *not* over. Climate catastrophe is beyond denial. Intersecting injustices are being unveiled every way we turn, and it is becoming clear how tightly woven into the fabric of our society they are, and how comprehensively things need to change if we are to right these wrongs.

The modern media landscape renders knowledge of all the world's suffering inescapable. In the words of Lutheran minister Nadia Bolz-Weber:

> I just do not think our psyches were developed to hold, feel and respond to everything coming at them right now; every tragedy, injustice, sorrow and natural disaster happening to every human across the entire planet, in real time every minute of every day. ... I'm not saying we should put our heads in the sand; I'm saying that if your circuits are overwhelmed there's a reason, and the reason isn't because you are heartless, it's because there is not a human heart on this planet that can bear all of what is happening right now.[1]

So often when I am confronted with the ills of the world, or (much closer to home) the struggles of my own life, or the life of the communities and institutions of which I am a part, a simple phrase comes to my mind: '*It doesn't have to be like this.*' It's a simple phrase but a powerful one,

---

[1]   https://thecorners.substack.com

because so often the temptation is to be fatalistic: to assume that the way things *are* is the way things *have to be*. But it doesn't have to be like this. We could – collectively – organise our lives, our institutions, our societies in a way that better serves the common good. In a way which serves human flourishing and the health of the planet.

I often think about this in terms of a 'God's-eye-view' – because God-language, God-imagery, works for me. I wonder what a world shaped by God's vision of love and justice would look like. And how we might get there from where we are now. What might it require of us? (If God-language doesn't work for you, it's an easy enough switch to think of the 'Highest Good': what would a world that was organised for the Highest Good look like? What does it require of us?)

That's the context, that's the upturned world: *upturned* in the sense of the disruption to our sense of what is normal, through Covid and climate change and an increasing awareness of systemic injustices – and, too, in the sense of its being, in many ways, an inversion of how we might intuit the world ought to be.

So why are we here? What is the particular mission of our Unitarian community in the world as it is today? What is our deep sense of purpose, our higher calling? What contribution can we make? What mission can we collectively get behind, feel a sense of ownership of, get fired up by?

I realise that language may be a barrier here, and that there will be hesitancy among some about embracing the idea of *mission*. Let's not get tripped up by language, as we so often do; let's not get distracted from what really matters. Call it our purpose, or our 'why', if you like. But let's own it as a *sacred* purpose – a *holy* 'why' – because we are a *religious* community. Our mission, our purpose, our 'why' will be rooted in our spiritual and moral vision. So let's own that. It is not – and should not be – just like the dry mission statement of an NGO. Let's articulate a vision which spells out what it is that we are ultimately here for. If nothing else, it's a useful lens through which to view, and evaluate, our choices about what we are doing, and how. If we have a clearer sense of our 'why', our purpose, our mission, and if we hold this ideal before us, keep it front-and-centre in all our decision making – whether personal, congregational, or denominational – it will shape everything we do. It is important periodically to ask ourselves: *Why* are we doing this? Does this particular course of action, or way of doing things, really serve the mission? Even if it is 'what we've always done'? This sort of mission-centred reflection may, in changing times, lead us to see that some of our forms and practices need to adapt in order to truly fulfil our purpose as a religious community.

In a way, this is all preamble, prior to putting my own cards on the table, mission-wise. My sense of why we are here, what we are meant to be doing, as a religious community, is echoed in a reading that we heard earlier, taken from a work by Tom Owen-Towle and recalling events in the USA in 1965:

> Dr Martin Luther King Jr summoned people of faith to Selma, Alabama, to create a righteous ruckus. His nonviolence was tough-minded and strong-hearted. It resisted wrongdoing and challenged sloth. King's mission was clear. As he said, *'The end is reconciliation; the end is redemption; the end is the creation of the Beloved Community'.*

> Hundreds of Unitarian Universalist civil-rights campaigners journeyed to Selma, Alabama, charged by their local churches to engage in this holy work. These stewards of justice knew that the Beloved Community is rarely embodied in any one place, time, or group, but ever stretches its embrace to include outsiders, strangers, the humiliated, and the marginalised.[2]

2   Tom Owen-Towle, *Growing a Beloved Community: Twelve Hallmarks of a Healthy Congregation* (Boston: Skinner House Books, 2004).

For me, the heart of our mission is Building Beloved Community. For the first umpteen years of my Unitarian life I heard this phrase bandied about a great deal, out of context, and it took me ages to realise that I had not fully understood what it meant. When people were talking about 'beloved community', I thought they meant something like: striving to make our congregations nice, inclusive, welcoming places, where we play nicely and get along (not that we always manage to achieve even that). But now I realise that those words carry a lot more weight. To speak of the 'Beloved Community' (with a big B and big C) in the way that Martin Luther King famously did is to hold up a vision of a world transfigured by love and justice: the world as God would see it.

There are many other names that gesture towards much the same vision. Take your pick: the Kingdom (or Kin-dom) of God ... Shalom ... Paradise (if you've read Stephen Lingwood's great book on Unitarian mission).[3] Perhaps you would prefer to characterise it more simply as 'a Better World'. Each of these images has its own resonances, and some may appeal to you more than others; but again let's not make the mistake of getting hung up on the language or allow the vanity of small differences to get in the way of discerning a coherent vision here: they all point towards a world where love and justice reign. A transformed world where all are liberated – set free from oppression in all its insidious forms – all of us enabled to live as our whole, authentic selves, and flourish in our fullness. What a dream!

If this vision of the Beloved Community (or the Kingdom of God, Shalom, or Paradise) is one that speaks to your heart's longing for love and justice and liberation – if you too have a sense, as I do, that this should be the vision that shapes our Unitarian mission – then we have to ask ourselves: What would this mean in practice? What would it *look like* for our congregations to be 'Building Beloved Community' (as I am

---

3   Stephen Lingwood, *Seeking Paradise: A Unitarian Mission for our Times* (London: The Lindsey Press, 2020).

sure many of us already are)? Consider this quote from Rebecca Parker, a prominent Unitarian Universalist / United Methodist minister. I find it particularly compelling and I have really taken to heart. She shares a vision of how our congregations can be

> 'communities of resistance' – counter-cultural habitations in
> which people learn ways to survive and thrive that can resist
> and sometimes even transform an unjust dominant culture ...
> an embodied experience of covenant and commitment ... which
> ground life in shared rituals that nourish and strengthen people
> spiritually, emotionally, psychologically and intellectually, providing
> a deep foundation for courageous and meaningful living.[4]

For me, this ties it all together: the sense that we are living in an unjust culture – but that 'it doesn't have to be like this'. That in small 'communities of resistance' we can practise a different way of living, in alignment with our values, and with that vision of 'Beloved Community'. Even if we are just a small, flawed, microcosm of 'Beloved Community', or an 'Outpost of Paradise', in such communities we can tell the truth about the grief and the overwhelm that we experience – and we can gain insight and courage from the journey that we make as companions. We can practise grounding our vision of love and justice and liberation in the messy but meaningful reality of living alongside other mixed-up human beings in all of their – *our* – glorious complexity. Showing solidarity and offering practical support as we each attempt to live wisely and well.

This sort of community does not arise by accident. It takes intention, care, and sustained work. That phrase used by Parker – *'counter-cultural'* – is important. There are so many magnetic forces in the prevailing culture that pull us back towards *un*just and *un*loving ways of being.

---

4 Rebecca Ann Parker, 'Life Together' in *A House for Hope: The Promise of Progressive Religion for the Twenty-First Century* by John A. Buehrens and Rebecca Ann Parker (Boston: Beacon Press, 2010), p. 37.

And these forces are often really subtle: ingrained habits of being, ways of thinking that are hard to unlearn, and also material realities that constrain our life choices and drain much of the energy that we need for resistance.

Often in our communities the most privileged still hold most of the power; the loudest voices dominate the conversation and drown out the tentative offerings of the quiet ones. Institutional inertia means that we often *'do what we've always done'*, so we *'get what we've always got'*. (We are often blithely unaware of all the barriers to participation for those who do not fit the mould.) We talk a good game in terms of diversity, but, without examining our practice, the words are empty.

It's an aspiration. It is hard to live out this vision in practice. To create a culture that goes against the grain. But if we are to live out this vision, build 'Beloved Community', make our congregations 'Outposts of Paradise', then we need to consciously, doggedly, break away from prevailing norms. And key to our mission, as I see it, is the sacred practice of intentionally creating 'safer, softer, kinder' spaces. And spaces that are more just, more equal, more truthful – spaces where every voice is heard – where we resist privilege, redistribute power, practise consent, and give up on pretence, so that all can be authentically present as we truly are.

I have experienced flashes of this reality, from time to time, in our Unitarian communities. Most often at Summer School, in fact – possibly (let's be honest) because it's easier to live up to such high ideals if you know you've only got to hold it together for a week in August; but also in congregational engagement groups and gatherings such as 'Heart and Soul' sessions. Now is probably not the moment for me to evangelise at length about the transforming power of engagement groups (but I will just say that, for me, these small groups are the key spiritual practice by which we Unitarians might make this vision a reality). The key intention of such groups is to cultivate right relationship with self, with others, and with God (or however you prefer to characterise that larger reality which grounds and holds us all). At their best, these groups are carefully structured to be counter-cultural 'communities of resistance' which break the habits of behaviour that we have learned from the wider culture and, in doing so, model a better way of being. They involve group covenants which shape how we relate to, and make space for, each other; and simple rituals and structures which ground us in a bigger reality and remind us of the overarching spiritual purpose that we share. In these groups we are called back to our highest intentions and are supported to realise our mission.

If you are not used to this sort of practice, engagement groups can feel clumsy and awkward – at first. You might feel terribly self-conscious once all your default conversational habits are interrupted. But in time you will notice that quiet voices start to get heard, invisible struggles get seen, people start trusting each other with the deeper truths of their lives. These are places where we can be our whole selves: bringing our grief and sorrow, our hopes and joys, our messiness and confusion, and feel safe in the sharing, as we know that we will be held in compassion and loving-kindness. We can bring concerns about the suffering and injustice in the world, and our sense of overwhelm, and find the strength and solidarity – and sometimes practical help and support – to go on. And in my experience the quality of relationship that we develop in such groups – and the habits of thought, and behaviour, and care – slowly ripple out and exert a wider influence. The conscious effort towards creating right relationship starts to come naturally, and the culture shifts: first the culture of the congregation, but then – in small, humble ways – ripples *will* spread beyond.

This is just one vision – one that is especially close to my heart – of how we might characterise our mission, and how we might begin to build the 'Beloved Community' through small group practice. And our team of speakers will present more visions, at greater length, in the week ahead.

To close, I offer some words, borrowed (slightly adapted) from Starhawk, the American author and activist: words that perhaps speak to this vision.[5] May they inspire us as we journey onward together. She writes:

> Community means strength
> that joins our strength to do the work that needs to be done.
> Arms to hold us when we falter.
> A circle of healing. A circle of friends.
> Someplace where we can be free.

Amen.

....

The author

Revd Dr Jane Blackall currently serves as Ministry Coordinator with Kensington Unitarians (Essex Church). Jane is the convenor of the Hucklow Summer School panel and has been a regular member of the organising team since 2005. She is a long-standing advocate of the transformative power of Engagement Groups and Small Group Ministry and is the creator of 'Heart and Soul' contemplative spiritual gatherings.

....

5   Starhawk: *Dreaming the Dark: Magic, Sex, and Politics* (Boston, Beacon Press, 1982, 1988, 1997).

Questions for reflection and discussion

1. Think about some of the issues that have troubled you recently in your personal life, in your church community, or in the life of the world. What issues make you think *'it doesn't have to be like this'*? Focus on one or two issues that you feel especially called to engage with more deeply in the context of your church or local community.

2. How might a sense of dissatisfaction with the-way-things-are be calling you to bring about the change you wish to see in the world? Is there some small project you could initiate to address the issue, perhaps in your church, or in your local community? Or an existing project that you could support, engage with, take inspiration from?

3. Rebecca Parker calls on our congregations to be *'communities of resistance'* in which we can learn to survive and thrive in ways that defy the dominant culture and its injustices. What practical steps might you take towards building a *'community of resistance'* in which we might embody the Kingdom/ Paradise/ Beloved Community?

2 What Is the Spirit Saying to the Churches?

Jo James

Introduction

The kaleidoscope has been shaken. The pieces are in flux. Soon they will settle again. Before they do, let us re-order this world around us.[1]

We must all have had some sense of wishing to make a new start out of the chaos of the pandemic, to *build back better*, adjust to *a new normal*, to re-order things in a more equitable way. And yet this felt sense that '*the pieces are in flux*' is worth considering with care.

The opening quote (above) is actually taken from a speech by Tony Blair at the outset of the Afghan war; and, as Naomi Klein has persuasively argued in *The Shock Doctrine*,[2] chaos can be a tool of manipulation in the hands of the powerful. We should look closely at the dismantling of '*our NHS*' during the pandemic even while the health service was being applauded from the front doorstep of 10 Downing Street, and we should take care before we assume that we are in a state of positive change from which boundless possibilities must inevitably emerge. We might be aware instead that this is a dangerous place and a hazardous time. Not all of the ideas and trends that are emerging now are benign, and as a faith group we might find inspiration from our sister church in Transylvania which, under Soviet occupation, took as its motto: 'Be as cunning as snakes and as gentle as doves' (from the Gospel of Matthew).

---

1 Tony Blair, Speech to the Labour Party Conference, 2/10/2001.
2 Naomi Klein, *The Shock Doctrine: The Rise of Disaster Capitalism* (Toronto, Alfred A. Knopf Canada, 2007).

What is religion?

I want to begin my contribution to this collection of Summer School talks from a deceptively simple perspective and ask: *'What is religion?'* Discovering some perspective on this question may lead us to an inquiry into how we respond to our past, and I hope then to point out ways in which unacknowledged histories may influence current realities, and perhaps to identify potential pitfalls, before offering what might provide an alternative prospect.

In the Study of Religion as an academic discipline, the definition of religion is itself contentious. At the risk of over-simplification, I would suggest that there are basically two main camps into which definitional analysis divides. The first category is Substantive (or essentialist), consisting of those who think that religion should be defined by its 'essence', what it centres on, raises up, or brings into focus;[3] so, according to this perspective, the rituals and (crucially for Unitarians on all sides of the debate) the *beliefs* of adherents become of primary importance. And the second category is Functional (or instrumental), consisting of those who think that religion should be defined by its 'activities', what it 'does': the *actions* of its adherents which can be identified objectively by research into data.

But both perspectives in this debate have a big problem: if your definition is substantive and you say that what religion centres on is *belief in the supernatural* or *worship of a deity*, you then erase, or at least fail to acknowledge, traditions which require no belief in God or gods, or experiences of the supernatural; and therefore certain types of Buddhism (especially western secular Buddhism), Jainism, and Taoism, for example, and certainly some Unitarians, just won't fit into your definition – yet what they do is, I would say, certainly 'religious'.

---

3   I am heavily reliant here on a brilliant article by Steve Bruce: 'Defining Religion: a Practical Response', *International Review of Sociology: Revue Internationale de Sociologie*, 21, 107–120 (2011).

But, on the other hand, if your definition is functional, then certain traditions, although outwardly seeming similar to evidently religious faiths in providing moral and emotional sustenance, comfort, instruction, and social cohesion, are clearly not religious; they might be guilds, mutual societies, educational establishments, dance-culture 'tribes', well-being groups, etc. etc.

So then you might instead claim that an activity is religious by virtue of quantifiable actions such as holding their gatherings at a given time and a special place, singing or chanting, wearing certain significant types of clothing, repeating rules, including significant rules which are available only to an elect or which an outsider couldn't possibly guess. This may sound rigorous, but I've just described a football game, which is not reasonably defined as religious.

And anyway both of these kinds of definitional analysis are over-reliant upon linguistic concepts at the expense of directly lived knowledge, wisdom, and experience; and so they risk producing a 'one-sided and overly rationalistic caricature of religion'[4] in the very place where a reliable and useful definition is urgently required. Because distinguishing religious from non-religious activities, events, and beliefs, and demarcating where the boundaries between them lie, remains key to understanding religion. According to Talal Asad, 'defining what is religion is not merely an abstract intellectual exercise ... [it] is embedded in passionate disputes'.[5] Passionate disputes on this very matter may indeed be seen to erupt from time to time among ourselves as Unitarians, despite the fact that our own *idea of ourselves* includes the ideas of freedom of conscience, reasonableness, and tolerance of the views of others. Something is clearly going on here which makes the subject uncomfortable, or even unbearable, so I must tread with care and compassion as we proceed.

<hr/>

4   Beverly and Brian Clack, *The Philosophy of Religion: A Critical Introduction* (Cambridge: Polity, 2008), p.4.

5   T. Asad, *The Cambridge Companion to Religious Studies*, ed. R. Orsi (Cambridge University Press, 2011), p.39.

Because, before asking 'Why are we here?', I'd like to ask, in the spirit of affirmative inquiry, seeking the best, the most positive aspects of the presence of our Unitarian movement in the world: 'What are we doing right now?' ... Then: 'What *could* we be doing?'... And then, maybe crucially: 'Does any answer to these questions really resolve the question "*Why are we here?*"?'

What are we doing right now?

So before asking you for your answers, I will say a little about mine in relation to the chapel that I serve. What are we doing? Aside from holding regular acts of worship, here in Leeds city centre our Mill Hill Chapel has funded and helped to run a Well-Being group for four years, a gently facilitated therapeutic group based on reciprocity and conversation. During this time we have also set up and helped to run a Conversation Group for Refugees and Asylum Seekers, to facilitate English learning and community cohesion. And we have set up and run a 'Spiritual Reading and Inquiry Group' within the congregation, to deepen our understanding of philosophy, theology, and each other through encounter and conviviality.

Does 'the art of conversation' in these different forms represent our closest approach to discovering a religious practice? Does this model perhaps relate to the historic 'salons' that earlier generations of Unitarians populated, and so provide a degree of congruence with our tradition, as well as a clear contemporary application?

Then there is our holding space for other religious groups. I have a clear appreciation of the historical Unitarian understanding that no single religious tradition has a monopoly on religious truth, but at the same time I don't subscribe to a naive pluralism. I have a standpoint of my own, based on my personal history, background, tradition, and location, so instead of attempting to lead services from a multi-faith perspective, I have offered space to other liberal religious groups to run their own activities: we have for the past few years hosted a Buddhist Sangha, a Sikh Simran meditation, and Muslim Jummah Friday prayers, all running independently at Mill Hill. We have also offered space to artists and arts students, hosted recitals, concerts and gigs, readings, lectures, theatre, performance and art works, live recording and filming.

What could we be doing?

Looking into the future, now that during the pandemic many of our activities have been curtailed, changed, or stopped completely, should our spaces host all sorts of lively arts (now so threatened by de-funding)? Might our chapels, meeting houses, and churches be reinvented as rehearsal and concert centres to come to the rescue of bands and theatre groups? ... Or should we develop the model of well-being groups and conversational practices? ... Or be hubs for all sorts of complementary therapies and meditative resources? Are we 'spiritual health centres'?

Or should we strengthen our social-justice campaigning activities? We had success in advocating same-sex weddings: should we now refocus on our campaigning history as inheritors of some of the great social reformers of the past? Should we lobby Parliament for a Universal Basic Income? A four-day week? Decriminalisation of recreational drugs? Should we campaign on behalf of refugee rights? Or against the destruction of the natural world?

Deeds or creeds?

All our ideas (howsoever good, exciting, progressive) fall into the 'functional' definition of religion, don't they? They remain firmly in the concrete realm of what we *do*. They enable a clearly instrumental definition of our role and place. And that may be agreeable to many here; we often say we are about 'deeds not creeds', or that it is our values, not our beliefs, that define us.

But I want to worry at these nostrums a little. Are creeds really the opposite of deeds? Setting aside the fact that intuition of the divine or holy does not necessarily imply a credal formula, are our deeds not in fact derived from, or inspired by, our lived orientation anyway? And is a sense of direction not an important human value which arises from our felt sense of the Holy? Certainly the great theologian of twentieth-century Unitarianism, James Luther Adams, thought that the relationship had to work this way round: that outwards from a sense of the Holy our communities could extend responsibility into the civic realm.[6]

The American anthropologist Clifford Geertz maintained that some rationalist attempts to explain religion disguise a desire to 'explain away' religion. Geertz instead viewed religious traditions as cultures that carried patterns of meaning, or *'systems of symbols'*, in order to transmit meaning from generation to generation and beyond generations.[7]

Beyond generations and between time: I want to take this opportunity to consider the word *liminality* here, at the mid-point of this talk. It derives from the Latin word *līmen*, meaning 'a threshold'. Liminality, according to Wikipedia (which seems as good a source as any), is

> the quality of ambiguity or disorientation that occurs in the middle stage of a rite of passage, when participants no longer hold their pre-ritual status but have not yet begun the transition to the status they will hold when the rite is complete. ... During a rite's liminal stage, participants 'stand at the threshold' between their previous way of structuring their identity, time, or community, and a new way, which completing the rite establishes. ...
>
> During liminal periods of all kinds, social hierarchies may be reversed or temporarily dissolved, continuity of tradition may

---

6   *The Essential JLA: Selected Writings of John Luther Adams*, ed. G. K. Beach (Boston: Beacon, 1998).
7   C. Geertz, *The Interpretation of Cultures* (New York: Basic Books, 1973).

become uncertain, and future outcomes once taken for granted may be thrown into doubt. The dissolution of order during liminality creates a fluid, malleable situation that enables new institutions and customs to become established.[8]

As long-time outliers, heretics, inhabitants of the borders, dwelling between humanist and Judeo-Christian spaces, both spiritual and religious, as travellers in the liminal – shouldn't we Unitarians be able to bear spaces of complexity more easily?

Our tradition of humanistic, reason-based, but clearly religious enquiry derives from the huge tumult of the Reformation in the sixteenth and seventeenth centuries. I spoke earlier of times of danger when the kaleidoscope is shaken; but these convulsions of culture are zones where our Unitarian tradition has historically flourished. Our earliest inception might be sited in the upheavals of Lollardism in England from the late 14th century onwards, or the subsequent revolutionary activities of Jan Hus in Bohemia, and those rebellions provided fertile ground for the Protestant Reformation led by Martin Luther; but (as George Hunston Williams pointed out[9]) the Reformation had a right wing and a left wing. The conservatism typified by Calvin and Luther was mirrored by the liberationism of the radical Anabaptists and the warm humanistic spirituality of the Socinians from which our own tradition grew, first in Poland and Transylvania and then in the United Dutch Territories: close enough to cross-fertilise into Britain in the period known as the English Civil War. That revolution galvanised the first wave of thinkers who were explicitly named Unitarian; and the next British revolution a century later – the Industrial Revolution – galvanised another wave, when Joseph Priestley and Mary Wollstonecraft visited revolutionary France, and Theophilus Lindsey and Iolo Morganwg seeded Unitarian churches

---

8   wikipedia entry https://en.wikipedia.org/wiki/Liminality (accessed 30/11/2021).
9   George Hunston Williams, *The Radical Reformation* (London: Weidenfeld and Nicolson, 1962).

throughout England and Wales. A century later, the 1840s' Age of Revolutions galvanised the most productive wave yet, as thinkers such as Anna Laetitia Barbauld, Harriet Martineau, James Martineau, and others oversaw the most influential period of revolutionary growth.

Acknowledging our shadow

We must not be afraid of times of great change. In the words of Father Richard Rohr,[10]

> Untarnished mirrors receive the whole picture, which is always
> the darkness, the light, and the subtle shadings of light that make
> shape, form, color, and texture beautiful. You cannot see in total
> light or total darkness. You must have variances of light to see.

Against the (admittedly slightly grandiose) portrayal of the revolutionary 'Epic of Unitarianism' that I have just presented, it is important that we also keep in view our shadow. I want to return to the Unitarian idea of itself and ask you a question. Try to respond quickly; don't over-think this: *Are you reasonably happy to be described as a 'non-conformist'?* And now another question: *Are you reasonably happy to be described as a 'Puritan'?*

I suspect that 'non-conformist' is a label that you are happy to apply to yourself – but 'Puritan'? Not so much. And yet 'non-conformist' was simply the new description ascribed to Puritans after the restoration of the monarchy in 1660, following the failure of the English Revolution and Civil War. And if it is true that religious traditions are 'cultures which carry patterns of meaning', or *'systems of symbols'*, as Clifford Geertz says,[11] then we must assume that we also bear relationships to our Puritan history.

---

10   https://cac.org/category/daily-meditations/2021/
11   C. Geertz, *The Interpretation of Cultures* (New York: Basic Books, 1973); see also
     T. Asad, 'Anthropological Conceptions of Religion: Reflections on Geertz' in *Man,*
     New Series, Vol. 18, No. 2 (1983).

And the reason why I mention this is that perhaps the reason why we seem to fail to manage these liminal spaces well, why we seem unable to bear boundaries and borderlands, when you would think that these current turbulent times should be – really ought to be – our natural territory, is because part of our Puritan inheritance is an over-reliance on *rectitude*.

A Puritan might be assumed to value purity, right? Virtue, righteousness, so perhaps affirmation of our own rightness: this continual emphasis on our rectitude might be why we so frequently cross over, in our disputes online and elsewhere, into regions which are '*hot*', uncomfortable, or even unbearable. Because if being right is our highest value, if we allow our unacknowledged shadow identity to be our dominant characteristic, then, as we decline and become smaller and increasingly hollowed out from inside, as we rely more on our own members to provide all our needs, and gain less from outside, we will grow more and more likely to resort to puritan habits like purity standards, moral formulae, or ethical codes by which to impose conformity; more likely to accuse each other of heresy and ostracise rule breakers, more likely to engage in in-fighting, more likely to indulge in increasingly frequent purges based on the transgression of rules and codes. We will dwell less in liminality and borderlands, less in thresholds and more in confines: spaces of clarity, certainty, and supposed truth.

Recovering our sense of the sacred

But is there not an alternative possibility? What if, instead of the puritanical over-reliance on the virtue of rectitude, we were persuaded instead to re-connect with the sense of the holy, the sacred or numinous that our spiritual and mystical inheritance also allows us to affirm? If we were to re-centre a personal sense of connection with the ineffable, with the infinite, and with the eternal as our core orientation, a sense of self-possession despite uncertain times could be given space to emerge: a recovered sense of self which facilitates ambiguity and flexibility, which allows for and engages with nuance and subtlety, which acknowledges the right to exist alongside difference and discomfort. A sense of personal spaciousness and spiritual resilience could transform this diminished sense of ourselves.

One of our signboards at Mill Hill reads: *'Spiritual resistance to the temper of our time'*, and I know that other ministers in our movement are working on contemplative and mystical forms of practice which seek to reconnect with that spiritual side of our religious inheritance. In this they are reconnecting with a valid and valuable element of Unitarian tradition which runs in and out of our past like a thread that appears and reappears in a tapestry through Anabaptist, Socinian, and other European radical reformation ecclesia, through the philosophers of Deism and Transcendentalism, the 'spiritualisers' of the Victorian era, and on into our own period, where Beloved Community threatens or promises to abolish the difference between the human community and the divine spirit. And it is possibly in this abolition of boundaries between the human and divine that we are able to perceive most clearly the theological points of contact between Anabaptist thinking, Deist belief, liberation theology, and contemporary Unitarian thinking.

So, what is the spirit saying to the churches? My title is taken from Chapter 3 of the Book of Revelation, a mystical text of rare power which is one of the remaining texts of one of the earliest Christian communities which, it is thought, emerged and formed around the apostle John. It is from that context that we also have this luminous fragment:

> Beloved, let us love one another, because love is from God; everyone who loves is born of God and knows God. Whoever does not love does not know God, for God is love.[12]

---

12   I John 4: 7 and 8.

The author

Revd Jo James has been the Minister of Mill Hill Unitarian Chapel, Leeds, since 2014 and is currently a member of the Executive Committee of the General Assembly of Unitarian and Free Christian Churches. He studied Ministry and Theology at Oxford and the Study of Religion at Cambridge in preparation for ministry, and contributed to the Unitarian Theology conferences in 2016 and 2017. Before ministry he worked in the theatre for more than twenty years. He is married to Ann, a ceramic artist; they have two young children, three cats, and a dog.

Questions for reflection and discussion

1. How does what we love affect our orientation in the world?

2. What spiritual practices do you engage with in congregation?

3. What spiritual practices would you like to explore in congregation?

4. What is 'spiritual well-being', and how might it manifest in our congregations?

5. What would make you 'come alive'? or How can we revitalise what we love, and do what we love, instead of doing what we feel we ought to?

---

3 Our Mission: To Be An Inclusive Spiritual Community

Shana Parvin Begum

Introduction

This talk will pose more questions than it answers. My offering is really me having a conversation with you, and I invite you to receive it in that spirit. It's not a 'to-do' or 'to-don't' list, and it's not meant to be a rant either. This is a focused time for raising awareness of some difficult issues, in the hope that it will spark ideas and prompt communities to take action. This is an offering from my heart, in the hope that it touches yours.

I had a rather negative reaction when I learned that *mission* would be the theme of this year's Hucklow Summer School. After my initial reaction ('What would I know about "mission"?'), what came to my mind was the damage done by conventional Christian concepts of mission and their exclusionary effects. The erasure of other people's identities makes them feel that, in order to gain acceptance, they must deny or abandon their heritage, their culture. Even when minority groups were invited to come to Britain, like the 'Windrush generation' in the 1950s and 1960s, they felt that they had to conform to a society and a culture in which they did not necessarily feel comfortable. And they had to practise in secret what *was* comfortable for them.

I have been thinking about the diversity of lived experiences. Reflecting on 'exclusion', these questions came to my attention:

> *Who and what are we excluding, and how can we be more inclusive?*
> and
> *How can we truly become a beloved community that welcomes all?*

Reflecting on 'mission', my attention moved to my own inner self and my personal experiences. The things that I am longing for, the things that I think could be better, and how we can change the culture in which we as Unitarians dwell, to create a community where people can be unapologetically themselves. So this is what I hope to do: share ideas, thoughts, feelings, and wisdom with you from the place where *I* stand.

I will be referring to internal and external realities, inner and outer diversities, how we engage with ourselves, with people around us, with communities and the world. Because our welcome should not be just about inviting people in: it is also about going out and engaging with our surroundings, our world, working in the community, supporting other organisations. When I talk about welcome, I don't just mean how we greet people: it's also about how we might create safe and diverse spaces, places where people can find meaning and a sense of belonging.

Unitarians 'recognise the worth and dignity of all people and their freedom to believe as their consciences dictate'; and an Object of our General Assembly is to promote 'the service of humanity and respect for all creation'.[1] The principles of the Unitarian Universalist Association in the USA affirm the inherent worth and dignity of every person; justice, equity and compassion in human relations; and acceptance of one another and encouragement to spiritual growth in our congregations.[2] I will focus on these three principles.

The worth and dignity of every person

My first-ever job was working in retail as a sales assistant, wearing a uniform that consisted of a pink twin-set and ill-fitting trousers. I started out in the shoe department and I was OK there, but my sales figures were

---

1   www.unitarian.org.uk/who-we-are/radical-spirituality.
2   www.uua.org/beliefs/what-we-believe/principles

particularly poor in the clothes department. I am no good at lying, and in order to make a sale I just could not tell someone they looked good in the clothes they were trying on, even when they didn't. When my colleagues ignored a certain shopper, for example a teenager wandering into the store, I would be the one who served them, just as I would serve anybody else, because everyone is worthy of receiving the same level of customer service. Although my sales figures weren't always the best, I was someone whom customers would ask for or seek out. Even after I had left my job, customers would ask 'Where's Shana?'.

In the language of that retail environment, a shopper is someone who might look around, buy something from you, then leave, and you may never see them again. They had got what they needed. But a customer is a shopper with whom you have developed a relationship of trust. They will return to your place of business the next time they need to buy something. Different people have different needs. As Unitarians we should be aware of that fact. How often do you hear comments about newcomers such as 'I sat with them for 20 minutes, I gave them tea, and they didn't even sign up for the newsletter'; or 'They said they were interested, but they didn't show up to the meeting of the Book Group'?

We sing the hymn 'Come, Come, Whoever You Are', affirming that *everyone* is welcome, even if they stay only for a moment and then leave. It is based on a poem attributed to the 13th-century Sufi mystic, Rumi:

> Come, come, whoever you are.
>
> Wanderer, worshipper, lover of leaving.
> It doesn't matter.
> Ours is not a caravan of despair.
> Come, even if you have broken your vow
> a thousand times.
> Come, yet again, come, come.

Our doors should always be open. And when people do enter our spaces, remember that they don't have to be physically sitting in our circle to be part of a circle of love. Wherever a person feels comfortable is absolutely OK: the chair at the back or in a corner, or a cushion on the floor. We can acknowledge them with a warm smile, without needing them to sit next to us.

If we genuinely believe in the inherent worth and dignity of each person, then we need to remember that people are not numbers – existing only for raising membership totals, or newsletter sign-ups. We are a spiritual movement, a religious movement. Our mission should not be all about numbers. Yes, numbers are important for keeping us going and sustained, but that will happen naturally if we meet people where they are, no matter what is dwelling in their heart, or the shape of their mind, or their body, or how their spirit rests in that body.

'I'll scratch your back if you scratch mine': I don't like the implications of that deal, especially in a spiritual context. We need to move towards selfless giving, genuinely serving humanity. The transaction should be between an individual and their inner self. In an internal transaction between you and what you hold to be most sacred, the receiving is a sense of being whole, a sense of joy, and a sense of fulfilment. Discrimination of any form creates a hostile environment. A safe space needs first to be welcoming, letting people know that they are valued, heard, seen: a message that needs to be clear and evident.

Poor leadership, whether due to incompetence, or to abuse of power, or insecurity, can create toxic conditions. We need to make sure that people are feeling creative, motivated, and inspired to carry on doing the work. Volunteers are key to our churches, but what might happen if they feel overworked, as often is the case when a few people are doing the bulk of the work or are undervalued? I invite you to think about devloping good practice by looking at what you are already doing in your congregations, and what might need improvement in order to create a healthy community.

You might like to create a 'Workplace Well-being Charter'; you can find information about this on the internet.

Disabilities – visible and invisible

In conversation once with someone who said they really wanted to attract more young people to their congregation, I had to ask *Why? What is the intention?* Is it because the long-standing members are tired, and you need younger people to come in and do the jobs that others have been doing for 10 years? The tired treasurer, the tea maker, they've had enough? But you are assuming that a young person is fit and healthy and willing and able to take on the roles that need filling. I have lived with a health-limiting condition for more than half of my life, and it is frustrating when people assume that I am OK just by looking at me. Even after saying I am unwell, I still get asked to do stuff.

In London we have badges saying 'Please offer me a seat', which vulnerable passengers can wear on public transport. A friend got one for me after witnessing the impact that a long journey had had on me. I had been meaning to get one, and I had mentioned as much to someone during a group conversation; their response was 'Why do you need one?' – like I couldn't possibly need support. My reason is nobody else's business, but the fact is that unless your condition is visible it is really not seen. This is why some people wear sunflower lanyards now: to show that they have a non-visible health condition; it's not about being excused from wearing a face mask during the pandemic.

When our buildings are not accessible to people with disabilities, it sends the message 'We didn't think of you as part of our community'. And remember: disability takes many different forms. I wish I could have studied British Sign Language at school, instead of (or as well as) French. It is not fair for those with hearing loss to have to rely on lip reading, and, unless a speaker is a careful enunciator, words can be misunderstood. When I have enquired about the presence of a BSL interpreter for Sunday services, I have been told 'We don't have anyone who needs it'. I am glad that on-screen closed captioning is available for these Summer School talks, even if it is only 80 per cent accurate.

Unitarians were leaders in the struggle for equal marriage. The Marriage (Same Sex Couples) Act was passed in July 2013, and the first church weddings of same-sex couples took place in the following year. We should be proud of that fact. But did you know that getting married, or even cohabiting, cancels a disabled person's eligibility for financial support from the State, thus putting them in a vulnerable position? And according to SafeLives, a domestic-abuse organisation, disabled people typically experience abuse for an average of 3.3 years before seeking support, compared with 2.3 years for non-disabled people. After receiving support, disabled victims are 8 per cent more likely to continue to experience abuse. Is there really marriage equality if people with disabilities can't get married without losing their income, benefits, or health insurance?

If we truly affirm the intrinsic value of every person, regardless of identity, we need to include every individual, and make sure that nobody is an island. Access to our spaces, regardless of disability, is an issue that we as organisers should think about ahead of time. It is about having support structures in place to enable people of different abilities to do the things that they need to do. Do we wait for needs to arise, or do we ensure that we have means available so that people are able to access our spaces as and when they arrive? We can't always know what people need unless they tell us, but we should at least be creating a context where people feel safe to speak up and let us know what they require. Yes, adjustments require money, and it is easy to say 'We can't afford it'. But what message does that send? As a community we need to put pressure on our leaders. We need to ask what we *can* do. What resources are available? Can we start a fundraiser?

When someone is physically ill in hospital, it seems relatively easy for others to know what to do: bring their loved ones flowers and get-well cards to lift their spirits and help them recover quickly. But when someone opens up about their psychological challenges, maybe their specific struggle with suicidal thoughts, they may be labelled or even shunned. They may lose their job, relationships, respect, sense of self-worth, and more. Official statistics show that one in four people will experience mental-health difficulties of some sort in any one year. That would suggest that we each know someone who is living with challenges to their mental health. According to the Office of National Statistics, 21 per cent of adults experienced depressive symptoms in early 2021, more than double the ratio before the Covid-19 pandemic. Loneliness and isolation are real, and the lockdowns have had a devastating impact on many people's emotional well-being. A lack of understanding, support, and access to mental-health services makes facing challenges even harder. As Unitarians, with our broad and diverse offering of worship, wisdom, and practices, I feel that we are well placed to offer solace to those seeking acceptance in a spiritual community. But when people enter our spaces, we also need to practise empathy. It's a super-power.

Welcoming younger people

Our world is always changing, Our lives are full and busy, and we need space to rest, however we show up. Does your congregation create unconscious expectations that members should wear their Sunday best when attending services? Do you frown upon the use of contactless donations during or after services? (OK, technology can be a bit frustrating when we are gathered for worship, but think about it: we are connected by Zoom right now!) We need to create space for younger people to explore spirituality, especially in this 'upturned world' in which we live now. There might be people who have moved to a new city during the pandemic lockdown, now exploring and needing community, spirituality, nourishment. We could be making an intentional offer of a healing space. Let's not focus on what we want from them: their presence alone should be enough.

Respecting ethnic and racial diversity

Our cultural upbringing and our personal experiences affect how we perceive and interpret what is put before us. If we are actively involved with issues that minority ethnic people have to deal with, we might attract more diverse congregations. We must recognise that racial inequality continues in many forms. For example, the Police, Crime, Sentencing and Courts Bill is highly racialised and will have serious ramifications for black and brown communities, and Muslim communities, as well as explicitly criminalising Gypsy, Roma, and Traveller communities.

But Unitarianism is rooted in whiteness and a particular socio-economic status. To quote from an address delivered at the General Assembly of the Unitarian Universalist Association in 2000 by Revd David E. Bumbaugh:

> When Theophilus Lindsey founded the Essex Street Chapel in England in 1774, the faith he offered attracted the middle-class and included amateur scientists and scholars like Benjamin Franklin. Priestley's Unitarianism grew out of the rigorous intellectualism of the dissenting academies and was a movement of the merchants and scholars and the literary class. It included people like Priestley, and Josiah Wedgewood, and Charles Dickens and Florence Nightingale and Neville Chamberlain—none of whom were representative of the laboring classes. Unitarianism in England was the creature of a middle class as it reached for respectability and access to power and influence.

David Bumbaugh went on to suggest that Unitarians' class identity may be less the result of wealth than a consequence of the educational levels that they have attained and value. What defines Unitarians as a movement may be their particular style of worship, a peculiar spirituality, based on those dominant educational levels, rather than a distinctive theology.[3]

---

3   https://files.meadville.edu/files/resources/vi-n2-bumbaugh-reflections-on-class-in-the-history.pdf

Our predominantly white congregations can be a challenge for some. Extra work needs to be done to create safe spaces, with intention. If a group or event is set up to cater specifically for black, indigenous, or minority ethnic people, it should not be regarded as a segregationist initiative. Such spaces are necessary for healing. Part of our mission could be doing much more outreach work in the community and creating connections that will bring in a diverse range of people.

In this country there are also poverty-based and class-based divisions that require a lot of work to be done. We have seen how the pandemic has hurt the most vulnerable people. Last year 2.5 million people used a foodbank; that's over 600,000 more than in the previous year. As Unitarians we should pay conscious attention to the question of where to invest our resources.

In the battle with the deadly Covid virus, society may have forgotten the outbreak of Ebola in 2014. It took five years for a pre-exposure vaccine to be developed and made available. *Five years.* In contrast, vaccines for Covid-19 were manufactured within ten months – because, of course, the virus affected the privileged. When the Delta variant was raging through India, was the impetus to provide vaccines driven by a genuine concern that Indian lives are worth preservation – or because the existence of Covid in India meant that it posed a threat to the affluent West?

Listening to diverse voices

How are you listening and responding to the voices that need to be heard? Listening can be hard. Political leaders don't do what they tell us to do, so it is not surprising that we can't be bothered to listen. But let's take a couple of steps to make our community a better place, one based on dignity and respect, where we pledge to listen to diverse voices. Our words and silences are powerful: they have the ability to heal, and equally they have the ability to cause great harm. Telling someone that they are being 'too sensitive', for example, can undermine and devalue their experiences.

It is important for people to be in control of the language employed to express their experiences. When we ask people questions as a way of getting to know them, we need to consider our intentions, and ask open questions with care. If someone refers to their 'husband', use the word 'husband'; if they have a partner, use 'partner' back. Making assumptions about people can be hurtful. Asking a widower about his wife may re-ignite his grief. Enquiring about children when a person has none might make them feel inadequate, or guilty that they don't want or can't have children.

Avoiding assumptions

One of the advantages of being on Zoom is that we can include our pronouns on the screen alongside our names if we wish, and it avoids the risk of misgendering someone else. Misgendering is addressing someone by using language that does not align with their affirmed gender: referring to someone as 'she' when that person identifies as male, for example. In the real world, unless people have name tags, we need to ask. I know that for some this may feel daunting, haunted by the fear of getting things wrong. But mistakes are OK. Just accept when you are corrected, apologise for your error, and know that you will do better in future.

Our individual experiences of the Covid pandemic have been unique to each of us. It has been restricting, but it has offered liberation too. Liberation from the need to go out and spend money in order to socialise. With everyone at home, there was more time and space for international connection. Because of social distancing, people check before entering another's personal space, giving permission for those who don't want anyone in their space to say 'no thanks'. The pandemic should not be an excuse: we need to ensure that asking for and granting consent becomes part of our nature and is taken seriously. So continue seeking permission to enter someone's space, including that person whom I mentioned earlier who wishes to sit quietly at the back. And to say that the pandemic is over is not OK if a person wants to continue being cautious.

Further thoughts about consent: when a person agrees to something, it doesn't mean we can take it for granted that they will do so next time: a 'they said yes last time' sort of attitude. Consent needs to be sought every time; names and pronouns need to be validated whenever we are checking in at a group meeting, or asking something of a person. When we offer the 'pass' option, let's mean it, because when someone is quiet, or 'passes', it doesn't mean they are not engaged. If someone says 'no', they mean no; persuasion is not helpful and can make people feel very uncomfortable. Everyone has the right to feel safe, whether from a virus, or from a person, a place, or a situation. That right should be respected. During our opening service, Jane Blackall mentioned the value of engagement groups. They always form a big part of Hucklow Summer School, and I would recommend attending one, or learning more about them, so that respectful practices become part of our everyday lives.

Recognising signs of distress

I encourage facilitators to consider deeply the manner in which discussion groups and meditation sessions are held. People have varying degrees of tolerance. Some are survivors of trauma, and being pushed too far to engage with something like a meditation, especially if lights are low, can be profoundly disturbing for them. You might like to research 'windows of tolerance': a term coined by neurobiologist Dr Daniel Siegel.[4]

Using grounding and mindfulness skills sensitively can help people to remain in the present moment. Those of us who lead worship, facilitate groups, or minister to a congregation are not necessarily practitioners of psychological well-being; but people seeking spiritual spaces often attend from a place of distress, usually a form of loss. There is no time for me to explore the topic of grief healing in this talk, but I will say that

---

4   David A. Treleaven and Willoughby Britton: *Trauma-Sensitive Mindfulness: Practices for Safe and Transformative Healing* (Norton & Company, 2018).

sometimes sitting with people in their suffering, in silence, is one of the most comforting things that you can do. And if there is a real concern, you might need to offer a signpost to another professional; it's always good to know local contacts in mental-health services, and in an emergency (it goes without saying) you should call 999.

Including children

Children and young people are rays of light and hope: they are the future. We should always make sure that we do enough to welcome them, keep them, and grow with them. But to help children to manage their needs and emotions, first you must learn to manage your own.

If children are restless or upset, do we regard their carers with disapproval? (I say 'carers' because we cannot assume that the adults accompanying the children are their parents.) Are families genuinely encouraged to be comfortably together in your chapel service? In those congregations that don't have separate children's activities, how are younger people accommodated? Could we offer support with a nod, a smile, a gentle bit of encouragement to let the carers know 'It's OK', 'You're doing great', maybe even 'You're courageous to be here with your children' – because some people feel too embarrassed to be out with children who become unsettled. But you know what? They are children. As adults we have an average attention span of 20 minutes. (I know that means I might be talking to myself at moments during this address. Some of us just can't keep our minds and bodies still. It does not mean that we are bad or don't want to engage. It's not something to take personally.)

Welcoming the marginalised

The people with the loudest voices get heard the most: whether their words or behaviours are right or wrong, their visibility is noticed and responded to. We need to give voice to the silenced, the ones who sit in the corner at meetings, who probably have something profound to say. Take note of who is speaking up – and who isn't. Are we including those people whose voices have not been heard: a person of colour, a person with disabilities, those who identify as LGBTQ+, those living with mental-health challenges, people who are neurodivergent? We need to make sure that those people are invited – not just to speak at a meeting, but to belong to our community.

Our Unitarian forebears were persecuted for their liberal religious ideas. Although they were mostly white middle-class men, many from privileged social backgrounds, they were still marginalised for their liberal religious views. We should honour the fact that our history began with the experience of persecution – of being treated as 'heretics', having to hide, having to flee their homes; and, as Jo James argued in his presentation, we owe it to those forebears to continue campaigning for the rights of marginalised people. I began writing this talk before the Afghan refugee crisis erupted, and I am holding a lot in my heart right now. I have been involved in a community sponsorship project: a refugee resettlement programme supported by local people in Hampstead, including Rosslyn Hill Chapel's social-action committee. I wonder if our Unitarian mission should include welcoming refugees, with each of us playing our part, whether by offering accommodation, or by doing personal activism on online platforms, petitioning the government to help.

No love without trust

In the short time that I have been involved in the Unitarian movement (even though it feels like a lifetime), I have been cautioned that it is a small community and *people talk*, so I guess there is a Unitarian grapevine that extends across the country: someone whispers, and it spreads everywhere. But if we feel the need to speak to others about the topic of the conversation, first we need to check what is OK to share. In the words of the spiritual teacher Radhanath Swami: 'There cannot be love without trust, and there cannot be trust unless we take responsibility to act in a way that people can trust us.' We should consult someone directly, rather than relying on hearsay, or on that grapevine.

We live in a time of 'cancel culture': that is when a person, usually a prominent public figure, is blocked from having a public platform or career because they have said or done something deemed to be offensive. I would like to bring that closer to home. When there are disagreements, take a moment to contemplate what is happening for you. What does it stir up? Why shouldn't that person be part of your congregation, attend your Sunday services, serve on your committee? Can we respond to challenging individuals without naming, blaming, or criticising? When we meet others from a place of curiosity, positive change can be created.

Of course, if somebody is becoming a hindrance to the vision of the community, preventing the congregation from fulfilling its mission, affecting its health, then action might need to be taken. I am not suggesting that we should just put up with everything. However, there are ways to proceed in such contexts. Congregations might consider having a set of rules for how to handle challenging situations: the decision should not be taken behind closed doors by just one person, or a few people. And if disruptive individuals have to leave, it's OK.

Healing ourselves

My wish is for us to be an inclusive spiritual community. One that feels truly welcoming and is constantly working to do better, and being accountable for the times when we fall short. But how can we begin to change ourselves and those around us in order to heal and reconnect? Pema Chödrön, an American nun in the Tibetan Buddhist tradition, says that in order to become more part of this world we are living in and less separate and isolated and afraid, what we need to do is

> start with loving-kindness for ourselves. As the barriers come down around our own hearts, we are less afraid of other people. We are

more able to hear what is being said, see what is in front of our eyes, and work in accord with what happens rather than struggle against it. The Lojong teachings [or mind training] say that the way to help, the way to act compassionately, is to exchange oneself for other. When you can put yourself in someone else's shoes, then you know what is needed, and what would speak to the heart.[5]

I used to want a pet tortoise. One of the things I like about tortoises is their ability to retract their limbs when feeling the need to withdraw. It reminds me to turn inwards and pay attention to the signals of my emotions, my body and my mind, and have a conversation with what rests in my heart. We all need to look deeply and wholly within ourselves in order to heal, to be truth tellers and justice seekers. By helping ourselves we can be a more inclusive society. In taking time to reflect and care for ourselves, we can become more self-aware, recognising our privileges, whether in the context of gender identity, or sexuality, or race, or ability, or socio-economic status. But we should also become aware of our shadows.

And we need to experience love, to rest, to allow time for enjoyable things. Things that make each day worth living, each moment worth living and being present in. Dancing, healthy eating, cooking, healthy sleeping patterns, playing, taking breaks, taking a deep breath, finding beauty in our day. When we are spiritually healthy, we can work to heal wounds. Remember that filling our wells, maintaining our inner peace, is not about getting to a finish line. It is about the journey. If we can appreciate the journey, the progress that we make, we can enjoy life. If we keep our energy levels high, others around us will charge theirs, and this is how we change the world.

---

5   https://www.shambhala.com/compassionate-actio-excerpt-from-start-where-you-are/

Closing words

May we be determined to do better, be better human beings. Creating a more compassionate culture. Going beyond religion and going into deep spirituality. It has been wonderful to be here with all of you magical beings, with our divine lights, spiritually connected together. May we continue to sow seeds of change, influence, and diversity, and enjoy the love that community brings. When the chalice is extinguished, may we keep the flame of love in our hearts, and may the light of that love shine on to others.

―――

The author

Shana Parvin Begum (she/her) is a Muslim Unitarian, currently a ministry student with Unitarian College. She has a background in media, has been trained in counselling and yoga, and loves working with children, to which she brings her passion for psycho-education and well-being. Shana is also a practitioner of Bhakti Yoga and was given the spiritual name Sri Devi by her Guru.

Questions for reflection and discussion

1. Think of a time when you visited a community space for the first time: either your own spiritual community, or any other community that you have visited. What made you feel welcome in that space? Or what made it not feel so welcoming?

2. What commitment can you make to move forward in creating safer, inclusive spaces?

3. Bring to mind a particular person, or group of people. How will you invite or welcome them, and what do you hope to learn from them?

4. Our Unitarian mission should be to create faith spaces that are truly inclusive. What are your thoughts on inclusion? Where are the gaps in your congregation and the wider Unitarian movement? How can we fill them?

4 'Fearless and Fervent Folk, Poems and Poetry, Songs and Suffering'

Rory Castle Jones

Introduction

In my talk I want to explore why, as Unitarians, Free Christians, and people of faith, we gather together in community. I will interweave my contribution with stories from the radical past of Welsh Unitarians, which may help to illuminate ways forward for us in the twenty-first century.

But before I delve in, here – for those who might not know much, or anything, about Unitarianism in Wales – is an extract from the history of Welsh Unitarianism written by Revd Dr Elwyn Davies, which has provided the title of my talk. He wrote:

> It can be said that Unitarianism in Wales is of a special brand because, although it reflects in mood and movement what transpired over the border in England and on the Continent, its character was moulded in the hands of a minority people whose every-day life was mingled with poems and poetry, songs and sufferings, and who could proclaim the newer ideas of Priestley and Martineau, Channing and Parker, in one of the oldest languages of Europe.

> The Unitarianism of the old agricultural counties of Cardiganshire and Carmarthenshire has always been tinged with a certain quality of unhurried stability that is only known to people who live near the soil; on the other hand, the Unitarianism produced by the

fearless and fervent folk of Glamorgan is tempered with vitality and enthusiasm only known to those who live by the furnace and the mine.[1]

And it is to those 'fearless and fervent folk' with their 'poems and poetry, songs and suffering' that my talk is devoted, because I believe that their stories can help us to discern our sacred mission in the twenty-first century.

Why are we here?

The question posed by the Summer School panel – *'Why Are We Here?'* – is the right one for us to be asking. For me, personally, I have been thinking about that question a lot recently, as I finish my ministerial training [Summer 2021] and look forward to my imminent ordination, when I will become a Unitarian minister – a vocation described by the late Revd Jacob Davies as 'the most glorious occupation a man or woman could ever desire'.[2]

Back in 1965, Jacob Davies, a household name in Wales for his radio and television appearances, addressed the Unitarian General Assembly's Annual Meetings in Swansea. In his powerful sermon, published subsequently by the Lindsey Press, Jacob Davies described the many challenges faced by British society in the 1960s – from declining church attendance to social breakdown, poverty and homelessness, and the terrifying threat of nuclear war. He declared: 'This is the moment

---

1   D. Elwyn Davies, *'They Thought For Themselves': A Brief Look at the History of Unitarianism in Wales and the Tradition of Liberal Religion* (Llandysul: Gomer, 1982), p. 28.

2   D. Jacob Davies, *Another Way to Unity? Challenge and Response. A Sermon preached by Rev D Jacob Davies at the Anniversary Service held during the Annual Meetings of the General Assembly of Unitarian and Free Christian Churches at Swansea in April 1965* (London: The Lindsey Press, 1965), p. 11. www.unitarian.org.uk/wp-content/uploads/2021/01/Challenges_and_Response_1965.pdf

of choice', telling his audience that it was a matter of challenge and response. The challenges were clear and numerous – the response was up to them.

Jacob Davies' message is as true today as it was in 1965. Some of the challenges faced then are still with us today. Others have faded, and other new challenges have emerged, like the terrible threat of global climate change. Many of the things predicted by Revd Davies about the future of the church have come true – and I want to use them now to sketch the context in which we, as people of faith, are working in Great Britain in the third decade of the twenty-first century.

Firstly, traditional churches of all denominations are dying, and the coronavirus pandemic has undoubtedly hastened that process. This is true for Unitarians as much as it is for other church denominations. Secondly, the old denominational divisions within Christianity have become irrelevant to the vast majority of British people. Many of the more successful churches are now mergers of different old denominations. Basically, people are not very interested in theological disputes over trifling matters conducted between increasingly shrinking denominations.

As Jacob Davies put it in 1965: 'The ordinary human being looks not for arguments that Unitarianism or Methodism is right, but for spiritual support in his never ending strife with adverse circumstances. There are no sects in a speeding ambulance; there is no division of humanity in a hospital ward at the dead of night.'[3]

Nevertheless, despite the growing irrelevance of those old denominational lines for most people, the diversity of theology and social attitudes within the Christian Church in Great Britain remains staggering. A particularly important area, which for many newcomers is an indicator of a church's

---

3   Davies, *Another Way to Unity?*, p. 7.

overall outlook, is its attitude towards transgender, lesbian, bisexual, and gay people. In this respect, contemporary Christian churches vary from the totally inclusive to the appallingly exclusive.

Thirdly, most people are not part of a church or religious community. The spiritual aspect of many people's lives is not fulfilled, but they certainly don't imagine that they will find what they need in old-fashioned churches and chapels, with their strong associations with sexist, homophobic, and bigoted attitudes.

And what about the wider context in which we live today? Our society is centred on work, money, and profit. We are doing enormous and perhaps irreversible damage to the natural world around us, causing changes to our planet that are wiping out entire species and will result in major problems for humanity, including refugee crises, conflicts, droughts and famines, and mass displacements of people.

And so, in this context, what are we – as people of faith, whether Christian or otherwise – called to do in the world? Why are we here? I want to explore some key areas of importance – telling stories from our radical past to help us find ways forward. These themes will include climate change, refugees, national identity, inclusivity, and community. I then want to show you a vision of what a Unitarian church of the future might look like, before drawing some conclusions about our mission and why we are here.

Climate change

First, I want to address what I think is the most important challenge facing us: climate change. And to begin, I want to take you to a small market town in south Wales 230 years ago. In the 1790s, in one of history's great periods of upheaval – the time of the French Revolution, and great radicalism in Britain – one of the founders of the Welsh Unitarian movement, the distinguished bard Iolo Morganwg, was running a shop selling books and other wares in the Welsh town of Cowbridge.

Unlike his competitors, Iolo refused to sell unethical goods, including sugar from the slave plantations in the West Indies. Controversially, in his shop window was a sign advertising treats made with sugar from the East Indies – where slave labour was not used – with the following words: *East India Sweets, Uncontaminated by Human Gore*. This shocking message, which must have stopped passers-by in their tracks, reminds me of the Extinction Rebellion protestors today, with their messages of *Tell The Truth*, *Act Now,* and *Join the Rebellion* – making people face the prospect of the extinction not only of animal and plant species, but of humanity.

One of Iolo Morganwg's famous slogans was *Y Gwir yn Erbyn y Byd* – 'The Truth Against The World'. Again, this reminds me of the Extinction Rebellion slogan, simple but compelling: *Tell The Truth*. Iolo Morganwg is said to have placed a book in his shop window labelled 'The Rights of Man'. At the time, Thomas Paine's revolutionary book *Rights of Man* was banned in Britain because of its promotion of dangerous ideas like democracy and liberty. And so, one of Iolo's many opponents rushed to the shop to purchase the book, hoping then to take this damning evidence straight to the authorities. But when he opened its cover, he was dismayed to see that the book labelled 'The Rights of Man' was, in fact, not a book by Thomas Paine, but the Holy Bible.

Having the last laugh as usual, mischievous Iolo had made the point that if we want to find a book advocating freedom, love, and justice, we need not look very far. We have the Bible at our fingertips. Surrounded by businesses profiting from the most appalling enslavement of fellow human beings, Iolo Morganwg took a stand and did things differently, backed up by the greatest book on the rights of humanity: the Bible.

Today, undoubtedly our greatest challenge is the climate crisis. And, for me, there is much to learn from Iolo Morganwg: speaking the truth to power, stopping people in their tracks, being unafraid to be controversial and unpopular if necessary. The climate crisis presents a practical challenge, but also an emotional, psychological, and spiritual challenge. It forces us to reassess not only how we live and work – but our faith and our theology too.

In the 1790s, a world without slavery perhaps seemed unimaginable to most Britons, just as a world in which we put nature and human well-being above human greed seems unimaginable today. I believe that our job, as people of faith, is to imagine the unimaginable. Frank Lloyd Wright, the great architect, who came from a prominent Welsh–American Unitarian family, famously said: 'I believe in God, only I spell it N.A.T.U.R.E.'

Refugees

Inextricably linked with the climate crisis is another crisis of our time: the refugee crisis – or, more accurately, crises – which Shana Parvin Begum addressed in her theme talk. Although people are compelled to flee their homelands for many reasons, as the impact of climate change is felt more and more, many predict that mass displacements and more frequent and dramatic refugee crises are coming. What role can we play in helping those forced to become refugees? And what can we learn from stories from our radical past?

One of the greatest Welsh Unitarians – and perhaps one of the least well known – was Rosalind Lee. We claim her as Welsh, because, although she was from Birmingham, she came to Wales in the 1920s, one of the early women ministers, and made her home near Swansea. A formidable woman, when sitting on the interview panel assessing new ministers, she asked only one question of the trembling candidates: 'Are you able to stand on your hind legs, young man?' As an English-born, female minister working in the South Wales valleys during the Great Depression, Rosalind Lee certainly knew the importance of ministers being able to stand up tall, with courage in their convictions, and she knew the importance of getting things done.

In the late 1930s, with the rise of the Nazis, Rosalind Lee left Britain for Prague, where she spearheaded the rescue of a large number of Jewish child refugees. Before and during the war, she campaigned tirelessly for offering asylum in Britain to Jewish and other refugees, in the face of often hostile and anti-Semitic reactions. In March 1939, on the eve of the Second World War and the Holocaust, writing from Prague to the British Unitarian movement back home, Lee appealed with these words, which echo down to us through the ages:

> In the name of humanity these unhappy people must be got away quickly ... Have we any right to sit by with folded hands and accept this as 'history'? Our ancestors had a reputation for humanitarian ideals and interest in civil and religious liberty. When the 'history' of this time is written, shall it be said that we looked on calmly ... or shall we be counted amongst those who put humanity first and practised their principles of world brotherhood? It is for us to decide by our action here and now what will be the verdict of history.[4]

Among the millions of Jewish victims of the Holocaust, and other targets of Nazi persecution, were many who had been refused asylum in Britain and elsewhere, even being sent back on ships and trains into the hands of their oppressors. In the midst of recurring refugee crises in our time, faced with the desperate needs of refugees from Syria, from Afghanistan, and elsewhere, Rosalind Lee's question from 1939 feels equally important today. What are we doing? What can we do? What should we do?

----

4   Rosalind Lee, 'Refugees in Central Europe' (March 1939), in Judy Hague (ed.), *A Century of the Unitarian Women's League 1908–2008: A Selection from the League Newsletter* (Sheffield: British League of Unitarian and Free Christian Women, 2008), pp. 101–2.

I think that we can draw on the Biblical imperative to welcome, feed, and clothe the stranger and to 'love our neighbour', and on the inspiring example of Revd Rosalind Lee, to help us find ways, whether great or small, to help refugees in our own local communities and around the world. I believe this to be possible because I see it happening already in some of our Unitarian churches here in Wales – and elsewhere in Britain too, in initiatives like the Ullet Road Church Rebels Football Club for refugees and asylum seekers in Liverpool.

National identity

I turn now from the refugee crisis to the question of national identity. A distinctive feature of Welsh Unitarianism is its strong connection to the Welsh language, culture, and collective identity. Many of our pioneering figures, such as Iolo Morganwg, Tomos Glyn Cothi, and Josiah Rees, played a hugely important role in shaping modern Welsh culture.

In tonight's opening sequence, we heard the song *Tân yn Llŷn*, about a key moment in modern Welsh history, when in 1936 three Welsh men who started a fire at the RAF Bombing School on the Llŷn Peninsula in north Wales in protest against militarism were sent to prison for their actions. In the twentieth century, many Welsh Unitarians started metaphorical fires of protest in their own way, in particular in campaigning for the Welsh language to have equal status with English after centuries of persecution and suppression. One such campaigner was Sali Davies, a teacher from Lampeter in the heart of the *Smotyn Du* – 'the Black Spot' – the Welsh Unitarian stronghold in Ceredigion. In the 1960s, Sali rose to national prominence when she took a stand for her civil rights and those of her fellow countrymen and women. After a long career in teaching, Sali retired and received her pension forms from the state. They were worded only in English, and she politely wrote back, requesting them to be sent in her own language, in Welsh. The state refused. And so Sali declared that she would live without her pension until Welsh-language forms were made available.

It was a small matter, but it was a point of principle and part of a wider campaign to demand linguistic and cultural rights which had long been withheld. Sali's case became symbolic of that struggle, and she won her case eventually, in 1966. It was just one of many battles which had to be fought over decades to secure recognition and support for the Welsh language. Her story can help us as we navigate the complex national identities of the four nations that make up the United Kingdom, as the union looks ever-more fragile and unsteady.

In the song that we heard earlier we find the words: *Beth am gynnau tân fel y tân yn Llŷn? Tân yn ein calon, a thân yn ein gwaith, Tân yn ein crefydd, a thân dros ein hiaith.* Or, in English, 'Why not light a fire like the fire in Llŷn? Fire in our hearts, fire in our work, fire in our religion, and fire for our language.' That fire is a theme running through Welsh history and through the history of Welsh Unitarianism – from its radical inception in the late 1700s, through the industrial revolution, and the painful struggles of the twentieth century. With fire comes danger and the potential for trouble, but fire also brings light, and warmth, and can guide us forward. One of our challenges today is to re-discover that flame.

Inclusivity

I want to say something now about inclusivity, a topic covered by Shana Begum in her talk, as she explored how our congregations can become truly welcoming, inclusive places. In particular I want to talk about the inclusion of lesbian, gay, bisexual, and transgender (LGBT+) people. Unitarians in Wales, as elsewhere in Britain, have been among the first religious groups to conduct same-sex blessings, then civil partnerships, and now weddings.

I take the liberty now of telling my own story: not to compare myself with the progressive Welsh Unitarians of the past, but to show how that tradition, developed over two hundred years, helped to produce some radically inclusive Unitarian chapels in Wales in the twenty-first century

– and how it can continue to do so. My own journey of faith is like that of many LGBT+ people. I was brought up in churches and chapels and Sunday Schools. And I loved the community, and the stories, and the message. Then I hit my teenage years, realised I was gay, and recognised that there was no place for me in the church or in any church – at least, any church that I knew of.

When I met my future husband in my 20s, he had a similar background and similar experience. We got engaged in 2015 and we both wanted a religious ceremony – which had become legally possible only the year before – but when we searched online we found just a handful of churches in Wales offering same-sex ceremonies. The nearest one to us was Gellionnen Chapel, a Unitarian chapel on an isolated hilltop not far from our village. We made a phone call, we ventured up there one Sunday ... and our lives were changed for ever. What we found was a chapel where we were truly welcome, where we didn't have to hide our sexuality or any other aspect of ourselves. From what I already knew about mainstream churches then – and from what I have learned during my ministry training – I see that this is gold dust. So few denominations offer such inclusion.

In his recent book *Black Gay British Christian Queer: The Church and the Famine of Grace*, Anglican priest Father Jarel Robinson-Brown writes: 'Am I loved? Do I have worth? Is my life worth living? These three questions are things that no human being should have to truly contemplate. Worse still to be driven to ask themselves, indeed the world, while simultaneously entertaining the very real possibility of the answer being "no". Yet these are three questions which I have in my own life asked myself.'[5]

Like Jarel Robinson-Brown, I too have asked myself those questions, as have many – perhaps most – LGBT people of faith. 'Am I loved? Do I

---

5   Jarel Robinson-Brown, *Black Gay British Christian Queer: The Church and the Famine of Grace* (London: SCM Press, 2021), p. 1.

have worth? Is my life worth living?' In the words of Father Robinson-Brown, telling LGBT people, particularly black LGBT people, 'that they are of value and loved by God is radical, life-saving and urgent work in a racist, transphobic and homophobic world such as this'.[6]

While I don't share his experience of being a black LGBT person, I do share the experience of questioning my own value and worth in God's eyes, because of my sexuality. This radical, life-saving, and urgent work – to tell LGBT people that they are loved and worthy of love – is, for me, a key part of my ministry. I count my blessings every day that I found an inclusive church and had my life transformed. I think it should be a key part of Unitarian ministry and mission. Registering a church building for conducting same-sex weddings is great. But it is the tip of the iceberg in building a truly inclusive church and inclusive denomination, as Shana explored in her presentation. We have a lot more work to do.

Community

I want to talk now about community. And to take you back in time once again, this time to the small Welsh village of Rhydowen, in 1876, when the Unitarian congregation and their minister Revd Gwilym Marles demanded the right to vote in accordance with their convictions, which for many meant supporting the Liberal candidate. The landlord, the Squire of Alltyrodyn, who owned the land on which the chapel was built, was a Conservative and was furious at their refusal to vote for his preferred candidate. And so he evicted them from their beloved chapel and from its graveyard, which held the bones of their ancestors.

The case immediately became a national scandal as a test case for the newly introduced principle of the secret ballot. The events in the village of Rhydowen became known as *Y Troad Allan*, the Great Eviction. On the

---

6   Robinson-Brown, *Black Gay British Christian Queer*, p. 1.

day of the eviction, the minister Gwilym Marles turned up at the chapel to be greeted by a crowd of three thousand Welsh women and men determined to defend their liberty, their faith, and their community. Gwilym stood with his back to the locked chapel and delivered one of the most important speeches in Welsh history, an impassioned defence of liberty, democracy, and freedom of faith. 'They can take our chapel from us', Gwilym told the crowds, bursting with righteous anger and fighting back tears, 'and they can even take our candlesticks' – but 'the flame and the light are God's, and that will live!'

For Welsh Unitarians like me, this was our Braveheart moment, when the eyes of the world were on a tiny Unitarian chapel in rural West Wales, whose congregation had taken on the powers-that-be, refusing to vote the way they were told, and contributing to a constitutional crisis which helped to entrench the principle of the secret ballot in British democracy. Just as Scottish hearts are inflamed at the moment in *Braveheart* when Mel Gibson screams: 'You can take our lives but you'll never take our freedom' and hurls himself at the enemy English, so when I hear those words of Gwilym Marles – 'they can take our chapel, but the flame and the light are God's – and will live!' – I feel inspired, emboldened, and alive. It's that flame which burns throughout our history and features in our symbols, our prayers, our hymns, and our imaginations. In the words of one of our greatest ministers, Elwyn Davies, it is 'the flame of truth and flame of love'.

Today, the Old Chapel of Llwynrhydowen is one of Wales' most famous and beloved chapels. Although we love our buildings – sacred places, houses of God – the story of Llwynrhydowen reminds us that the building is just stones and mortar. It carries within it the flame of faith, hope, and love when we light that flame within it, but it is the people – a sacred community – not the building that light and carry the flame. We need to be reminded sometimes that what is sacred is the community of people, not the building, however beautiful it may be.

A vision for the future Unitarian Church

From the radical stories of our past, I want to turn to the future now. What might the future look like for us? As Unitarians and Free Christians, as people of faith, as citizens of the UK, as members of the human race? In ten or twenty years' time, what might a Unitarian church in Great Britain look like? There are many visions of the possible future, and each of us will have our own visions, dreams, and prophecies. But here is *my* vision of one church in twenty years' time.

It might occupy a beautiful, well cared-for historic building, or a bright, attractive new space. In my vision, that does not seem so important. Because this church is focused on people, not buildings. It's a church that meets together, in various and diverse ways, every day of the week. In its own building, in the community space that it runs and makes available to the *whole* community, in its members' homes, in the café, in the pub, in the park. It's a church which has lots of fun, laughs a lot, and embraces adventure. It's also a church which takes faith seriously, which takes God, Jesus, and Christianity seriously, which takes other faiths seriously, and takes its mission in the world seriously.

There are services on a Sunday, when the church comes together to laugh and to cry, to be silent and to sing, to reflect, to pray, and to recharge for the week ahead. There are coffee hours, and pub nights, and social clubs, and support groups. There are kids' groups, and young adult groups, and groups for retired people. There is an LGBT group, a refugee group, a Welsh-language learners group. There is a radical Bible stories course, an Alcoholics Anonymous circle, a Buddhist meditation class, and a grief support group.

People in the local community bring their family and friends to the church to mark the important moments and milestones in their lives – births, marriages, and deaths. The church used to own two fields nearby. One is now a natural burial ground, where sheep graze. The other is now a fledgling forest, supporting nature and giving us fresh air. And because my imaginary church of the future is in Wales, its congregation are bilingual. The church has a hundred members. Some take part in lots of things, others take part in what they can. Hundreds more people use the building and participate in the church's activities.

The church takes a leading role in environmental work in the local area, conducting litter picks, tackling fly-tipping, educating children about nature, and working closely with those who work the land. In the preceding twenty years, the climate crisis has become increasingly important for this church, as they have seen an unrelenting sequence of disasters around the world: waves of climate refugees forced to flee their homes, some of them arriving in this area, and big changes in politics and business, as increasingly the population wakes up to the unfolding disaster on its doorstep. At the top of the agenda for every church meeting are the words 'Is this helping us to save the planet?', and every church service begins with a prayer for Mother Earth.

The Bible, with its ancient prophets and radical Jesus, is central to the life of the church, which seeks to build the Beloved Community here on earth: its members love their neighbours, forgive each other, share wealth, comfort the grieving, bring about peace, stand up for the poor, the oppressed, the downtrodden. Complementing the church's deeply held Christian faith, with its Unitarian focus on the oneness of God and humanity, but welcoming a broad range of theology, are the other faith traditions of the world, and the humanist tradition. It is a church based on love. It's a church which I believe is possible and which I hope and pray that I will live to see.

Conclusion

As we come towards the end of our time tonight, I want to return to that big question: *why are we here?* Well, I think – at the risk of sounding a little dramatic – that we are here to save the world.

The Japanese de-cluttering guru Marie Kondo, in her book *The Life-Changing Magic of Tidying*, encourages us to hold in our hands each item that we possess, whether it's an old sock or a treasured family heirloom, and to ask 'Does this spark joy for me?' If yes, great: hold on to it. If no, embrace the item, say 'thank you'– and then say goodbye. I think that if we are going to go forward as a Church, we need to embrace the Marie Kondo method. We need to look at everything that we do in church and in our movement and truly ask ourselves: 'Is this helping us to save the world?' If yes, great: keep hold of it and keep doing it. If not, say thank you and say goodbye – whether it's a deeply held tradition, a particular hymn book, a building, or a congregation itself.

And by 'save the world' I don't just mean tackling the climate crisis, although that is important. I mean saving the person crippled by anxiety and loneliness. The person desperate for community and connection. The young refugee family with nowhere to go. The LGBT person asking themselves 'Does God love me?' In this time of unparalleled danger, we need a church where we can cling together in fear and grief.

We need a church where we can work in unison to prepare to help those hit hardest. We need a church to change the way in which our entire civilisation functions, as it destroys our world and itself in its relentless pursuit of profit. We need a church which is both sanctuary and prophetic, both a safe haven and a voice of protest. We need a church which can draw on several hundred years of loving community, faithful prayer, and radical action – to hold aloft God's flame, like Gwilym Marles, in the face of a world gone mad – and offer hope, offer love, and offer a vision of a world fundamentally and radically different from the one in which we live today.

For me, as a Welsh Unitarian, I find strength, inspiration, and – importantly – challenge in the radical stories of our spiritual ancestors. Iolo Morganwg with his 'Rights of Man' Bible and campaign against slavery, Frank Lloyd Wright and his understanding of God as nature, Rosalind Lee and her courageous work with refugees, those who in the twentieth century pioneered LGBT inclusion, Gwilym Marles and his congregation's fearless opposition to the powerful and corrupt, and Jacob Davies, with his resounding message of hope.

I end with the words used by Jacob Davies to conclude his sermon to the Unitarian General Assembly back in 1965:

> Let us commit ourselves to the utmost for once, not that we may fill the churches with people but that we may fill our lives with meaning ... We are 'outward bound' on the greatest adventure we have ever known; 'outward bound' to intensify the awareness that there is a more abundant life awaiting humanity ... Are we able to provide the spiritual nursery for that eternal power of growth? Are we able to establish the Church of the Challenging Leadership, the Comforting Companionship and the Tolerant Fellowship? What say you? ... We are able! Then in the name of God, we shall![7]

Amen to that.

The author

Revd Dr Rory Castle Jones is the minister of Gellionnen Chapel, near Pontardawe in the Swansea Valley, where he lives with his husband and their dog. He has a PhD in History from Swansea University and left a career in Higher Education in 2018 to train for the Unitarian ministry. Since 2018 he has worked as part-time Communications Officer for the General Assembly of Unitarian and Free Christian Churches.

---

7   Davies, *Another Way to Unity?*, p. 11.

Questions for reflection and discussion

1. What are the stories of our Unitarian ancestors that we should be telling today, and why?

2. How can our radical past inspire us when facing the challenges of the twenty-first century?

3. Imagine your church or spiritual community of the future. What does your dream church in 2042 look, feel, and act like? What is it doing to save the world?

5 What If the World is Ending? What If It Isn't?

Kate Brady McKenna

Where we are isn't where we want to be

What should we do, as Unitarians, if it turns out that the world is ending? What should we do if it turns out that it isn't? How can we safely lament the collective and individual trauma of the last couple of years, and how do we find and share comfort?

> By the rivers of Bavel we sat down and wept as we remembered Tziyon. We had hung up our lyres on the willows that were there, when those who had taken us captive asked us to sing them a song; our tormentors demanded joy from us —'Sing us one of the songs from Tziyon!' How can we sing a song about ADONAI here in a strange land?[1]

We are living, I think you will agree, in a strange land. It looks the same, it sounds the same, but it is a strange, strange land that we are currently inhabiting. Our selves of two years ago would not recognise it, and we would not recognise ourselves from two years ago. What new ways of being we have found! Two years ago, which of us would have been familiar with dashing back into the house because we'd forgotten our mask? Which of us sneezed into our elbows in 2019? But which of us are now vastly better at asking for consent before any interaction with anyone?

---

[1]   Psalm 137, *Complete Jewish Bible.*

And two years ago, which of us could have pictured how we have conducted the annual Summer School this week? Which of us would have foreseen the widespread use of Zoom and, crucially, which of us would have imagined the power and the quality of the sacred space that could be created and held here, in virtual space? This last eighteen months has been one hell of a ride. And it's not over yet.

And I want to say something which I don't think has been said nearly enough. It is that even though this pandemic has happened to everyone, that does not mean that it hasn't happened to you as an individual, too. If you had experienced something so enormous and it had only happened to you, if just *your* world had been upturned like this, people would have been showering you with love and support, you would have been the focus of attention. I hope you *have* received love and support; but sometimes, as it must and should, the communal overrides the individual, and the individual can feel lost.

I wish I could say this to each of you individually, but of course that is not possible. But please hear this as if I were speaking just to you.

> I am so sorry for what has happened to you, personally, in the last eighteen months. I am sorry that your life – yours, as an individual – has been turned upside down, and that you, as an individual, have lived through that time in uncertainty, with grief, and with the exhaustion that we always forget grief brings in its wake.

> It hurts me that you, as an individual, weren't able to see your friends, your family, and your loved ones. It hurts me that you, as an individual, lived with the fear of you or they dying alone. It breaks my heart that you, as an individual, lived with grief and with the death of loved ones, and that you lived with it in a time where you weren't necessarily able to get the support and the ritual that you needed and deserved.

I weep with you that the big moments in your life were bypassed, or weren't what we need them to be. I am sorry for the things that have happened to you.

None of you needs my permission to do anything. But I give you my blessing here, and now, to sometimes take a moment to sit and mourn for what has happened to you, individually. For your own upturned world. I pray that you can find a safe time, and a safe space, to do that. To allow your own bruised soul, your own exhausted bones, and your own aching heart to speak to you and to be heard.

As a minister, I spend time hearing people's hurts. It is one of the huge privileges of ministry, whether that ministry is ordained, professional, lay, or completely informal. People let themselves be vulnerable near you, and that is an enormous and a sacred gift. People do bear their pain to you. People tell you what hurts them, what scares them, what they hunger for. All of those stories are precious gifts.

And almost inevitably, even after sharing huge pain and grief, people end by saying 'But there are others worse off than me'. This is one of many things which, repeatedly, confirm to me that people are brilliant: the fact that almost every conversation I have about people's pain ends with their concern for others reaffirms my conviction that people are brilliant, and that we are full of concern and love for others.

But you don't always have to add a caveat to your lament. Your lamenting, your grieving, your mourning is valid and sacred. When it is safe to do so, acknowledge your pain. Because your pain is part of your story, part of your song. Part of the song that you are asked to sing in this strange land. Tell your story. Sing your song. Our songs and our stories will be part of what might bring us comfort.

There is a piece of writing that I have loved for many years now: an essay called *Let Me Hold You While I May*, by the late Mary Jean Irion.[2] When I first came across it, in what now seem like untroubled days before Covid, but which we know had their own causes for lament, it seemed theoretical. Now, in its celebration of a normal, 'routine' day, it speaks to me just as strongly, but differently. Here is an extract:

> In time of war, in peril of death, people have dug their hands and faces into the earth and remembered this. In time of sickness and pain, people have buried their faces in pillows and wept for this. In time of loneliness and separation, people have stretched themselves taut and waited for this. In time of hunger, homelessness, and want, people have raised bony hands to the skies, and stayed alive for this.

> Normal day, let me be aware of the treasure that you are.

In late February or early March 2020, at the start of the pandemic, I realised that I have something that I now call *My 3am Theology*. It is a theology that is nothing like my rational, sensible, daytime, Unitarian theology. It is the theology that wakes you up, shaking and scared, and wondering if it is, really, the end of the world. The days of judgement. The end of time. Wondering if the horsemen are coming. Wondering if the story of the Ark was, after all, not a myth, not an allegory, but a piece of history that is about to be repeated. Wondering if all those people who stand on the street warning us that the end is coming, all those people on the conservative Christian Facebook pages from which I am mostly banned, might actually be right.

I mean, the world was actually on fire. The *seas* were on fire. The coastline was eroding: before our very eyes, sometimes. There were rumours, getting louder, about a deadly virus, getting closer. People were being

---

2   Mary Jean Irion: *Yes, World: a Mosaic of Meditation* (R. W. Baron Publishing Company, 1970).

displaced by war and hunger and poverty, and people seeking safety and sanctuary were drowning in the attempt. People were being unkind and untruthful about all of these things. And at 3 in the morning I often woke up and wondered if it was the end of the world. And then I would fall back asleep again, and in the warm light of day I would pick up my daytime theology again and carry on.

My 3am theology stung a little. There is a scene in *Buffy the Vampire Slayer* where Buffy is in a bit of a pickle at the hands of a baddie (for those who mind, it's Ethan Rayne), and he says to her: 'This will sting a little, but don't worry, that'll go away when the searing agony kicks in'. I wouldn't say that searing agony kicked in, but the slight sting of the 3am theology began going away and being replaced by a less sharp but more deep pain when it started pushing its way into my broad-light-of-day, wide-awake, 3pm theology as well.

Still rational. Still Unitarian. But getting a bit eschatological at the fringes. Because – and it is quite awkward for a Unitarian minister to say this to a mainly Unitarian audience – it still feels sometimes, doesn't it, as though the world is coming to an end. I don't think it all the time, of course, and I don't think I *really* believe it, but when I am having a low day, when I am unwell, when I am exhausted and in pain, then I do begin to feel it.

And it could be. It could be. It is not God's wrath, of course it's not. God loves us extravagantly, or God would not have brought us into being. Like Julian of Norwich's revelation about the tiny thing the size of a hazelnut, and the knowledge that God made it, God sustains it, and God loves it, we would not be here in our glorious variety and diversity if we were not worth it. Whatever the people with placards tell us, whatever the people on the conservative Christian pages of Facebook tell us, it is *nothing* to do with the fact that we are continually extending our understanding of the ways to love and the ways to be. Those people are wrong. There is no question there. (Although one of them recently called me a 'reprobate, entirely given over to my own lusts and desires'. Mate, you overestimate my energy levels.)

But we have certainly upset nature. If the earth wants to fling us off its very surface, who would blame it? Because much of this is our doing, and I'm not really at home to those who deny that. Climate change, the world on fire, the seas on fire, the seas rising, the coastlines eroding, and desperate refugees being left to drown? We simply cannot deny that we are helping all that along. Especially those of us who are privileged. Especially those of us who benefit from the sheer luck of living in the safer, wealthier parts of the world. You do know, don't you, that we are the camels that won't fit through the eye of the needle? We are the rich. So if Earth wants to evict us, I can see why.

What if the world is ending?

So let's just pretend, for a moment, that we found out, somehow, that the world – or human life – is coming to its end. Let's imagine what is both easy and impossible to imagine: that in a few hundred years we just won't be here. I am saying 'a few hundred' because I cannot bear to speak the actual possibilities here.

What do we do with that hypothetical and certain knowledge? What do we – as Unitarians – do to hold the world as sacred, given that knowledge? How do we serve a dying world, a dying population? What can we do?

What we have to do is we have to build a kingdom of justice and love. It is as simple as that. We are charged with building what I call the kingdom of God and you might call something else. We have a kingdom to build. If the world is coming to an end, we need to build a kingdom while it does so. Maybe that doesn't sound logical. If we knew the world was ending, couldn't we just give up and give in? Well yes, we could. But one of the few things I remember about school PE classes (apart from the crushing misery of the whole horrible affair) was one of the PE teachers saying, in some frustration, that you shouldn't slow down as you approach the finishing line, you should carry on running through it: run as fast as you can until the race is actually over, not until it's nearly over.

Actually an analogy that works better for me is one that the hospice movement holds dear: people are living until after their very last breath. We are alive until the very, very end, and we treat life with dignity and love and respect throughout. If you have ever sat with someone in their last moments, you will know this.

So we keep building the kingdom, even in the face of extinction. OK then. But how? You will have a million good ideas. I have a few to add to them. The Unitarian kingdom-building handbook should be a thing. A huge, glorious, collaborative thing.

First and foremost, we need to be there for people. I don't mean that in the glib, overused, *Friends* theme-song way. I mean we actually have to be there. We have to have a space – real or virtual, building or park or café – where we can be for people. And we have to make that space unimaginably flexible. We have learned, over the last eighteen months, that we can't simply sit in our churches on a Sunday morning and expect people to find us. We have to go where people are, and, increasingly, where people are is online, or in cafés, or, let's be honest, anywhere-but-church. We have to go to those places – as well as maintaining the presence in the church building, because we must not exclude those who yearn for that, either.

And we don't just need to 'be there for everyone', we don't just need to put a sign up saying where we are. We need to be overt and loud about our wish to be there, meaningfully and truly, for those who are not used to having a church be there for them. Please hear that: *we need to be there for people who are not used to having a church be there for them.* And you will note that I talk about our *wish* to be there. If we are going to be there for people, we have to know *how* they want us to be there. We can't just go 'Yeah, we're welcoming of everyone' without knowing what that welcome looks like – particularly to marginalised groups.

And we have to be there for people *in prayer*. Maybe you call it something else, but I am not apologising for the fact that prayer is central to me.

When we are there for people, we need to be there for them in prayer. prayer with them, prayer for them, and prayer that we may be granted the grace and courage to turn that prayer into something practical.

Why, as a faith movement, do we sometimes get embarrassed or even annoyed by that? Is it true to say that we are sometimes surprised and a bit anxious when someone says to us 'Will you pray with me?' I think more of us are OK with 'Will you pray for me?' (because we can do that in private); but 'Will you pray with me?' sometimes comes a bit harder. Let's start to practise hearing it. Let's start to practise saying it. Let's start to bring it into our spiritual and social vocabulary: will you pray with me? Can we pray together?

If a visitor comes into our space and asks us to pray with them, we need to be comfortable with that. If someone wanders into a church in need of an ineffable something, I think it's a safe bet that they are expecting prayer. If a visitor asks us to pray with them, they want us to pray with them, not offer them a chat about what prayer means to each of you.

Will you pray with me now?

> Let us turn to that which we hold the most sacred. That which
> nestles deep within the core of our being, and that which
> also surrounds us entirely. That which is intimately near and
> unimaginably far. That for which we have a thousand names, and
> yet for which there is no name.
>
> Let us feel the strength of that sacred power. Let us honour it. Let
> us know it to be sacred, and personal, and necessary. Let us hold
> it tenderly and lovingly, with thanks and joy. And let us know that
> it is mighty.
>
> And let us listen, deep within our hearts, to hear its message.
> Because it has a message. It is a message, and only when we truly

hear that message can we set about the work. And there is work to be done if we want to build a world of rightness and goodness.

Let us acknowledge our blessings. Let us acknowledge that we have all that we need to sustain life, and much that we need to attain pleasure. And in our gratitude, let us remember those who do not have these things, and let us pray for the strength to do what we are called on to do to set this wrong right.

Let us acknowledge that sometimes we do not do all that is within our power, that we allow others to suffer where we could aid them. That we sometimes cause that suffering. And let us know that every moment is a moment in which we can put our own failings behind us, know forgiveness, and move forward. If we only learn to forgive others, we have also learned to forgive ourselves.

And all of these things can be, if we make them be. We are how the world of glory, the power of love, and the kingdom of right and truth and justice will come into being.

Amen.

Who are we here for?

I found Unitarianism in a way similar to the way that Rory Castle Jones described to us in his talk. I was looking for a church to attend which would affirm and acknowledge my relationship with my then future-wife. She's now my ex-wife and one of the most important people in my life, so, had we but known it, we also needed a church which would support us as our marriage ended and our hearts broke: are we up for being supportive of that, when it happens, as well as for celebrating the joy of the wedding? We need to be.

If there had not been an overt statement that yes, our relationship would be affirmed, we would have assumed that it wouldn't be, and we would have moved on. It was that overt and unmissable acknowledgment that drew us in. Overt and unmissable and stated proudly and as officially as it gets in Unitarianism, in all sorts of places. That's why we joined.

And we should definitely be proud of that, as a denomination. Of course we should. But here is something that troubles me deeply: I fear that if someone who is Trans, or non-binary, or in a polyamorous relationship is looking for a faith community now, right now, this evening, I fear that they won't find a statement that they are welcome: a statement that we, as a denomination, have thought about them and want to offer them our presence and our love. It broke my heart when the motion on Trans rights was not chosen for discussion at the most recent General Assembly annual meetings, and I want to say to my Trans and non-binary siblings that I am sorry that we let you down. We need to build that into our kingdom.

And I mean it when I say that we have to be there *for people*. We have to be there *for them*. The primary reason for someone to join a spiritual community is for them to be spiritually nourished. When someone wants to join a faith community, I promise you they never think 'I'd like to try church because I quite fancy going on a tea rota and there's nowhere else I can get that'. They want to join a faith community because they need spiritual nourishment and spiritual companionship, and there really is nowhere else they can get that.

Someone does not have to become actively involved, does not have to join any committees, does not ever have to bring flowers or biscuits, does not ever have to do a reading, join a social group, or anything else. If someone comes along to our services – in person or virtually – for years and years and never even joins us for the social time afterwards, *we have to be there for them*. Let's not see everyone who comes along as a potential resource. *We* are the resource. We are there to provide the nourishment. Let's build that kingdom.

Right now, one of our priorities has to be to listen to people's fears. We listen to our own fears, we face them, we accept them, and we don't shout them down. And then we take the courage to listen to other people's fears, to face them, to accept them, and never shout them down. Who, when they are worrying about something, responds well to being told that they are worrying about nothing? When I am facing something medically terrifying, for myself or someone I love, I don't want someone to just go 'It'll be OK' (because I know that means 'Please shut up').

We need, as Shana Begum said in her talk, to sit with people in their suffering. We need to sit with them, not rationalise at them. We need to know, as she also said, that empathy is a super-power. We need to do everything in our powers to make our communities places where fears and uncertainties are not only allowed, but actively welcomed. I want us to be a church where people can speak of their fears, and have their fears heard. I want us to be a church where we never, ever, criticise or minimise someone's feelings of fear.

And if the world is coming to an end, we have to do what we can to lessen the harm. Even if, in this hypothetical situation (because, again, I cannot bring myself to say it is not hypothetical), where we know we have only a few generations left, surely we would want to make it as good for those who come after us as we possibly can? Surely that is a kingdom that we have to be building?

It really is not too late to ramp up our commitment to zero waste, to recycling, to not using our cars when we don't need to. Of course, as Stephen Lingwood has argued, those of us who are able to also need to be working to change the entire system that causes this crisis – but our micro efforts still matter. And it is definitely not too late for us to ramp up our commitment to improving the world for those of us who are the most marginalised, who are the most affected by what is happening.

What if, every time we make a decision involving a transaction, we stop and ask ourselves what impact that decision will have on the most vulnerable? What impact does your £5 car wash have on the person doing it for you, who might well be enslaved? What impact does your new iPhone have on the ten-year-old Congolese child who is mining the cobalt for it? What impact does your flight have on the inhabitants of the low-lying island that is going to vanish when the sea rises only a little bit more? What impact does your cup of coffee have on the coffee farmer whose weekly income is less than she needs to buy food for her family, let alone send them to school or to the doctor? What impact does your same-day delivery from Amazon have on the people who will have to pick it, pack it, and deliver it, and will still have to choose between topping up the gas meter or buying dinner?

Please know, as I raise these questions, that I am not preaching from a lofty position of perfection. I have an iPhone. I have used Amazon this very week. But if I keep asking myself the questions, it might inspire change. Paul Eddington, Quaker and actor, was once asked what he wanted his epitaph to be. He wanted it to say 'He did very little harm'. It is not too late to start minimising the harm that we will have done.

And here is an even bigger challenge for us: once we are used to doing that as individuals, how about if, every time we are going to make a decision in a church meeting, every single time, we ask ourselves what impact it will have on the most vulnerable? Yes, church meetings will be longer, but they will be more sacred, more prayerful, better contributors to the building of the kingdom. Where are we buying our coffee? Our toilet rolls? What form of energy are we using? What if there was a rule that every motion put before the General Assembly had to start and end with that question? What if our discussions were based around those questions, and what if we each voted according to the answer to those questions? *How does this affect the marginalised?*

There is an organisation that resolved to do this, to put the poor and the marginalised at the front of all decisions, and that organisation was the government of El Salvador in 2009. Inspired by the work of Oscar Romero, one of my spiritual heroes, the government of this tragically complicated and difficult country pledged to put the poor first in their decision making. We need to build that into our kingdom.

And it's not just purchasing: it's what we say, what we sing, what we read, and what we preach. What am I saying to someone who might want to join our church if all the hymns are from a European tradition and I think everyone will probably know them?

What am I saying when I deliver even a really good sermon about our sacred responsibility to support refugees and I talk about refugees as if they are only ever a 'cause' and not ever a part of our community?

What are we saying when we assume that someone can read the chapel newsletter? What are we saying when we fail to offer a large-print version of everything and an audio version of everything possible, because 'We don't have anyone who needs that'? What are we saying when our website is not accessible to people with sensory processing issues or sight problems?

What are we saying when we ask someone if they are married, if they have children, what they do for a living, where they live?

What are we saying when we blithely assume that someone can join us for that congregational meal out, or contribute to our charity appeal, or put a quid in the collection plate that we have just thrust in their face, or bring some food for the foodbank? What are we saying every time we use the word 'only' to someone when we are talking about money? *'It's only a fiver.'*

Much more to the point, what are we saying when people tell us that these things hurt and exclude them – and we ignore them and carry on regardless? What are we saying when a group tells us that we are hurting them, or contributing to their hurt, or at the very least not contributing to the easing of it, and *we carry on doing so*? What are we saying?

We have to question the impact of things. We also have to notice where that is a privilege: I can buy Fairtrade coffee, and avoid things that are made using exploitation, because I can afford the extra that it costs, and we have to know that not everyone can.

We need to tell our stories and sing our songs, even in this strange land. We need to revel in our history as individuals, and as a denomination. We need to revel in our non-conformist background – in our background which draws on both privilege and marginalisation, as Jo James pointed out in his talk.

Where is the comfort?

Where is the comfort here? The first comfort is that, even if the world is coming to an end, we can keep building the kingdom. We are all living until we are no longer living. We are not helpless. Our hearts can break, and we can still probably avoid despair.

The other comfort here is in some lines from a prayer that I will repeat in full at the end of this talk: the comfort here is in the words *'Be grateful, my soul. My life was worth living. Be grateful, my soul. My life was worth living.'* That is what would comfort me if the world were to be known to be coming to an end. That it was worth it. That our part in it – our part as a denomination, arguing the toss and speaking out for justice, and allowing freedom of thought and belief – was worth it. Our life was worth living. And that our own part in it – our part as an individual, holding doors open for people, and planting trees, and complimenting strangers on their hair or their dress or their child's behaviour, and moving out of the way when an ambulance needs to get past – was worth living.

We tell our stories and we sing our songs. And we keep building the kingdom. But do you know what? Sometimes, while Rome burns, we need to fiddle. I am not a great leader of a dying empire, and I don't play the fiddle, but over the last eighteen months my Candy Crush score has become either enormously impressive (or absolutely despicable, depending on your outlook). We need to play games, go to gigs, dance, eat toast, tend the garden, go for runs, play the fiddle, tell jokes, and watch terrible telly. We need to share the silly memes, we need to coo at pictures of each other's cats, and we need to just sit and stare into space.

And you know what, sometimes we may need to pretend it's OK. I do know these things sound irresponsible, but sometimes we need to turn off, turn away, and nestle into that which is simply comforting. It is healthy, sometimes, when everything isn't OK, to pretend that it is:

Buffy: Does it ever get easy?

Giles: You mean life?

Buffy: Yeah.

Giles: What do you want me to say?

Buffy: Lie to me.

Giles: Yes, it's terribly simple. The good guys are always stalwart and true. The bad guys are easily distinguished by their pointy horns or black hats. We always defeat them and save the day. No one ever dies, and everyone lives happily ever after.

Buffy: Liar.

And most of all, we need to bear in mind that our lives were worth living. Tell your stories. Sing your songs. Tell *our* stories and sing *our* songs.

What if the world isn't ending?

It is terrifying to think that the world – or human life on earth – might be coming to an end. We can't really conceive of it, any more than we can conceive of how the world will look when we ourselves are no longer in it. But something just as scary – actually, maybe even vastly more scary, because the hardest thing in this world is to live in it – is thinking about our life on earth going on for millennia more. And that is also possible. The sheer enormity of our responsibility – our responsibility right in this very second, because this stuff will not wait – is daunting.

Just say that we were to find out, without any doubt or question, that human life on earth has ten thousand more years to go. What do we need to do now, to make that future as blessed and as sacred as it can possibly be? What do we want our many-times-great-grandchildren to think of us? I have to admit here that, when I started planning this talk, I thought that the answers to the two parts of the big question were going to be very different. And it now seems to me that they are not, after all. It now seems to me that we have actions to take and stories to tell and songs to sing, and that we have to do them while holding two possibilities in our minds: that the world is coming to an end – and that the world isn't coming to an end.

The kingdom needs building whether we are building it only for the generation that is already here, or for four or five or 500 generations. You are possibly familiar with the Jewish proverb that says you know a society is healthy when old people plant trees that they will not see grow, whose fruit they will not taste, and in whose shade they will not sit. Let's plant trees. I mean, actually, let's do that. Physically and literally. But I also mean it figuratively, of course. Let's get rid of this 'Oh, it'll see us out' attitude to our churches, our congregations, and our denomination. Plant trees under whose shade we will not sit. And let's go a bit further – let's plant trees that might not even grow. Let's plant lots of trees so that some might.

We will be planting those trees in the rich soil tilled by our Unitarian forebears. We will be planting them in hundreds of years of progress and battle and courage. And we will be planting them knowing that the people who tilled that soil and who planted the trees under which we sit almost certainly would not like what we are doing now. I wonder what Joseph Priestley and James Martineau and Gertrud von Petzold and Norbert Capek would really think of us? And so we plant trees knowing that we probably won't like what the people who sit under them generations hence get up to. And we have to plant them knowing that it's OK. We will be planting them in hope, rather than certainty. But we should plant them.

This kingdom that we are building: we want it to be a kingdom of justice, of peace, of hope, of love. I want it to be a kingdom of prayer and a kingdom of God. And I want it to be a kingdom where, even if you are not people of prayer or people of God, you are still fully, entirely, wholeheartedly involved and centred in its structures. I want it to be a kingdom where people are inspired by all scripture – by which I mean by everything that is written – and by all traditions and by all sources. I want it to be, basically, a kingdom like in-person Hucklow Summer School.

Those of you have attended a Hucklow Summer School in person will know that it does offer a glimpse of that kingdom. I often say that Summer School shows us a picture of what Unitarianism could be at its very best, and that that shows us a picture of what the world could be like at its very best. Of course – as Jane Blackall pointed out in her opening address – some of that magic comes from the fact that the time at Summer School is limited to one intense week, and it is a fully catered, fully timetabled week, so we can all manage to keep up our kingdom building for that long.

I have friends living in permanent religious communities who acknowledge that community life is not always easy, that your sacred covenant with God and with each other does not mean that you don't get cross about who does the washing up, or irritated by each other's snoring. But it means that we can do it. We can exist in community, and we can build kingdoms. We can live in community and work, eat, pray, sing, talk, love, create, play, walk, and listen together. It is a thing that is possible!

What would the world be like if that idea could spread outwards? What would the world be like if we were all able to talk safely and consensually about our deeper truths, our theologies, the things that give life its true meaning? Let's build that kingdom.

Will you pray with me, before we leave? This prayer is by the Unitarian minister and martyr Norbert Capek, another spiritual hero of mine, who died in the gas chamber in Dachau in 1942.[3]

> It is worthwhile to live and to fight courageously for sacred ideals.
>
> Oh blow ye evil winds into my body's fire: my soul you'll never unravel.
>
> Even though disappointed a thousand times, or fallen in the fight and everything would seem worthless,
>
> I have lived amongst eternity.
>
> Be grateful, my soul,
>
> My life was worth living.
>
> I have lived amongst eternity.
> Be grateful my soul,
> My life was worth living.
>
> Amen

....

3   www.uua.org/worship/words/meditation/27762.shtml

The author

Revd Kate Brady McKenna has been the minister with Bury Unitarians in Lancashire since 2016. She trained for the ministry at Harris Manchester College Oxford, and at Heythrop College, University of London, where she gained an MA in Pastoral Theology. Raised more-or-less Quaker, she discovered Unitarianism in New England in 1999 and explored the faith further at the Octagon Chapel in Norwich a couple of years after that. Gradually she realised that she had a vocation for ministry. Her spiritual leanings are Christian and Pagan, and she delights in the ability to celebrate those influences fully. She is proudly Queer, a dog lover, and a fan of Buffy the Vampire Slayer.

Questions for reflection and discussion

1. How would you act if you knew the world was ending?

2. How would you act if you knew it wasn't?

3. What is our mission, as Unitarians, in this hurting world?

Lightning Source UK Ltd.
Milton Keynes UK
UKHW011439250222
399233UK00001B/24